The Authentic Counselor

The Authentic Counselor

Second Edition

John J. Pietrofesa
Wayne State University

George E. Leonard
Wayne State University

William Van Hoose
University of Virginia

Rand McNally College Publishing Company □ Chicago

Rand McNally Education Series
B. Othanel Smith, *Advisory Editor*

79 80 10 9 8 7 6 5 4 3

Copyright © 1978, 1971 by Rand McNally College Publishing Company
All Rights Reserved
Printed in U.S.A.
Library of Congress Catalog Card Number 77-77717

**DEDICATED TO
OUR CHILDREN**

*Ye are better than all the ballads
That were sung or said
For yo are living poems
And all the rest are dead.*
H.W. Longfellow

John David and Paul Pietrofesa
Melissa and Christa Leonard
Fred and Pam Van Hoose

Contents

Preface to Second Edition

Preface

Chapter 1. The Nature of Counseling   **1**

    Introduction   **1**

        Historical Antecedents of Counseling   **2**

        Counseling Defined   **4**

        The Goals of Counseling   **6**

        Counselor Goals   **7**

        Client Expectations   **9**

        Counselor Goals and Client Expectations: A Synthesis   **10**

        The Process of Counseling   **12**

    Summary   **16**

    References   **16**

Chapter 2. Focusing on Growth   **19**

    Introduction   **19**

Some Psychological Considerations of Self-Development   21

  The Self as Seen by Self   22

  The Self as Thought to be Seen by Others   22

  The Ideal Self   24

  Dynamics of the Various Self-Percepts   24

  Reinforcement of the Self-Concept   24

  Development of the Self-Concept   26

  The Influence of Needs   27

Implications for the Counselor   31

The Focus Upon Self-Actualization and Self-Concept   34

  The Self-Actualizing Person   34

  The Healthy Self-Conception as a Goal in Counseling   35

  Client Perception of Conflicts   38

  Inferring the Self-Concept   39

  Decision Making in the Interview   43

Summary   45

References   46

Chapter 3. The Counseling Relationship 50

Some Characteristics of a Counseling Relationship 52

Establishing the Relationship 55

Rapport 55

Special Considerations With Children 57

Trust 60

Empathy in the Counseling Relationship 60

Communication 62

Structuring the Relationship 65

The Real Relationship 66

Counselor Attitudes 66

Summary 68

References 69

Chapter 4. The Process of Counseling 72

Elements in the process 72

Counselor Expertise 72

Counselor Skill 73

Counselor Values 74

Counselor Responsibility to the
Counselee **76**

    Counseling — An Active Process **78**

    Counselor Behavior — Counselee
Resistance **80**

Establishing Security **91**

Transference **97**

Steps in the Counseling Process **98**

Summary **102**

References **102**

Chapter 5. Dealing with Ambiguity 104

Introduction **104**

    Ambiguity and Counseling Structure **107**

    Initial Phases of the Interview **109**

    The Self-Concept in Counseling **112**

    Later Stages of the Interview **113**

    Importance of Tolerance for Ambiguity in
Counseling **118**

Summary **120**

References **120**

Chapter 6. Authentic Behavior in the Counseling Relationship 123

Introduction **123**

The Need for Authentic Behavior **130**

Nature of Authentic Behavior **132**

   Definitions **132**

   Recent Research on Authenticity in Counseling **133**

   Self-Disclosure and Openness in Counseling **135**

   Dynamics of the Authentic Counseling Relationship **137**

   Pitfalls, or the "Authentic" Trap **140**

Summary **141**

References **142**

Chapter 7. Dimensions of Counselor Self-Actualization: The Fully Functioning Counselor **147**

Introduction **147**

   Emphasis on Experience **150**

   Rejection of Manipulation **152**

   Avoidance of Counselee Classification **154**

   Self-Expression **156**

   Satisfaction of Needs **157**

   Being as Well as Becoming **157**

Concern with Professionalization **158**

Playing the Role of Counselor **158**

Lack of Self-Consciousness **159**

Willingness to Accept Knowledge **159**

Counselor Moral Development **160**

Commitment **162**

Counselors as Models **162**

Summary **163**

References **163**

APPENDIX Counseling Practicum Handbook **166**

The Counseling Practicum **166**

The Counseling Interview **168**

Counseling Style **170**

Opening the Interview **172**

Purposes and Goals for the Interview **173**

Pace in the Interview **173**

Vocabulary **174**

To Advise or Not **174**

Closing the Interview **175**

Group Meetings **175**

Interview Logs **175**

Self-Evaluation **176**

Report Writing **176**

Confidentiality and Ethics **176**

Professional Growth **179**

Testing **180**

Use of Occupational and Educational Information **184**

Career Counseling **185**

References **186**

APPENDIX Informational Resources on Counseling 193

INDEX 201

Preface to the Second Edition

We have been quite pleased with the reception of the first edition of *The Authentic Counselor*. We had mixed emotions when asked to prepare a revised edition. The purpose of the first edition was to deal with the therapeutic ingredients of the counseling encounter. We feel that the original product is just as valid today as it was seven years ago. Yet, whatever hesitancy we felt to alter the book was far outweighed by an eagerness to improve on the initial work.

In 1971 we decried the dehumanized and artificial approaches to counseling. We are currently even more concerned, for the proliferation of gimmickry in the counseling field these past few years has been phenomenal—a gimmickry that substitutes for client growth, a game playing designed to keep the client coming back for more. Grandiose claims for questionable techniques and open disregard for ethics and morality in counseling are additional problems that continue unabated. This negative trend has not been as present in school counseling as it has been in private practice. On the other hand, the past five years have seen the development of training counselors in a systematic fashion, which undoubtedly has helped to produce more effective counselors than in the past. It is imperative for each counselor to develop precise human relations skills and, in fact, we identify these skills in the present edition. We feel it is just as necessary for the counselor to remember the importance of the ingredients of the facilitative relationship—a relationship founded in caring and a caring found in the heart of the counselor.

Each of the chapters has been updated with the latest research findings. We have extended certain sections and added some new material. The chapter on authenticity has been completely rewritten to reflect some of the negative ramifications of this dimension from a poorly prepared or unhealthy counselor.

We genuinely hope that readers will benefit from *The Authentic Counselor*—not just professionally, but personally, for it is that part of ourselves which we give in counseling that fosters the most growth in our clients.

We would like to thank our wives—Diana Pietrofesa, Helen Leonard, and Hazel Van Hoose—for their continued love and encouragement.

John L. Pietrofesa
George E. Leonard
William H. Van Hoose

Detroit, Michigan
1977

Preface

In order to be effective counselors, we need to be concerned with our own growth in our encounters with counselees. Certain therapeutic ingredients are crucial to the effective counseling relationship regardless of the specific school of thought.

This book is meant to deal with the therapeutic encounter—therapeutic not in the sense of therapy per se, but rather indicative of a facilitative, contrasted with a non-facilitative, relationship between two individuals. Counselors and counselees alike are disillusioned by dehumanized and artificial approaches to counseling. The lack of authentic responses by the counselor creates frustrations in both counselor and counselee. We take the position that a genuine partnership of counselor-counselee is necessary to understand the counselee's concerns. The therapeutic encounter can be painful for the counselor, for he/she has to discard prior securities and ego defenses to achieve mutual humanness. We propose to take a look at several ingredients of such intimate humanness within the counseling relationship. We hope this book may be of some value in graduate courses, in counseling processes and techniques, and also in the counseling practicum.

We would like to thank Miss Gloria Roppman for typing the manuscript, Mr. Jon Carlson for his comments and suggestions, and finally, our wives—Diana Pietrofesa, Helen Leonard, and Hazel Van Hoose — for their support and encouragement.

JJP
GEL
WHV

Detroit, Michigan
1970

Chapter 1 The Nature of Counseling

INTRODUCTION Within the past few decades the helping professions have gained a prominent position in American society. Counselors and psychotherapists who provide help to millions of clients—children, adolescents, and adults—are now found in most American communities and in a variety of social and private institutions. Counseling is not only sanctioned by the various states but is supported by a public that expects counselors and therapists to minister to the mental health needs of large segments of society. The individual who provides therapeutic assistance may be a counselor, psychiatrist, social worker, teacher, or minister. Formal preparation for the role of a helping person may range from a weekend workshop or a few courses in psychology to a doctoral degree from a university.

There is little agreement on what makes a "good" counselor or what constitutes successful counseling. There is general agreement, however, that counseling is a human relationship and that it involves a face-to-face interaction. Counseling also involves the values, attitudes, and philosophical concepts of humanness. As the counselor works, relates, and experiences with another human being, what he/she believes, feels, and displays in his/her behavior will influence counseling outcomes. Put another way, the counselor who wishes to be successful in helping clients will look beyond a knowledge of client behavior and counseling techniques. He/She will wish to carefully examine his/her own behavior in the helping process. This topic is given major attention in this book.

Historical Antecedents of Counseling People in need of therapeutic help have always been with us, but they have not always been helped. The mentally ill have been feared, tortured, incarcerated, pitied, and neglected. The maladjusted have been studied, analyzed, described, and often ignored. The plight of people with problems has been recognized for centuries. Yet it is only within the past century that serious attempts have been made to penetrate the vast area of an individual's mental and emotional existence.

The first concerted efforts to treat the abnormal were made by socially conscious and humanitarian individuals, and not by counselors, physicians, or social scientists. It was only after the disclosure of the pitiful neglect of the mentally ill that medical and social scientists became interested in the problems of mental health. The advent of psychoanalysis was one of the manifestations of this interest.

During the past century, and particularly within the past three decades, psychoanalysis has come of age and dramatic strides have been made in helping the mentally ill and the seriously maladjusted to find a more satisfying and productive life. Thus, the needs of persons with both developmental and incapacitating difficulties are recognized and the presence of over 100,000 helping professionals in the United States today (Van Hoose and Kottler, 1977, p.16) attests to the fact that efforts are being made to meet those needs.

Many people who need psychological aid are not mentally ill, nor are their problems as visible as are those of the seriously disturbed. Individuals who lead a personally unsatisfying life but who do not present problems for society often go unnoticed. People who are frustrated in their striving for goal attainment or who are unable to overcome obstacles in their environment may not have visible problems. Thus, they may receive no help until the condition becomes so severe that psychiatric aid is necessary. To be more specific, adolescents, striving in unusual and sometimes unacceptable ways to become whole people in their own right, are often censured and condemned, but seldom helped. Children suffering from incipient learning and behavioral disorders are sometimes punished and often ignored. Children or adolescents in a complex society attempting to answer such questions as "Who am I?" "What can I be?" or "What are my alternatives?" are not maladjusted, but their need for help is nevertheless evident. Counseling is a means for helping these persons confront and cope with such problems.

Counseling is a relatively new science concerned with helping people achieve better self-understanding and self-adjustment. It has deep roots in our democratic concern for the right and dignity of the individual.

The development of counseling as a method of helping individuals resolve difficulties and deal with life problems was directly influenced by Sigmund Freud and other psychoanalysts whose work stimulated considerable interest in emotional reality. The psychological testing movement and the emergence of guidance in schools during the first quarter of the present century were events that also contributed to the development of counseling. The writings of such people as John G. Darley (1937), Edmund G. Williamson (1939), and Carl Rogers (1942), although different in emphasis, helped lay the foundation for the modern counseling movement.

World War II had a significant influence upon counseling. Research studies and personnel work related to the war effort contributed greatly to our understanding of personality and adjustment. Rehabilitation of casualties with mental illness was a primary concern. Following the war, counseling programs for veterans provided extensive aid in helping the returning serviceman plan his future, overcome personal adjustment problems, and readjust to civilian life. The postwar period was also characterized by an increased interest in mental health and a renewed emphasis upon individual differences.

The rising interest in counseling in the late 1940s and early 1950s gave impetus to several moves to increase the professional qualifications of this service. In 1947, the National Vocational Guidance Association appointed a committee to prepare a statement on the preparation of counselors. The final report of this committee outlined a common core of training for all counselors. One of these core areas included not only the use of such tools and techniques as tests and the interview, but also the study of personality and the growth and development of the individual. A few years later the Division of Counseling Psychology of the American Psychological Association (APA) focused its attention upon the preparation of counselors (Van Hoose and Pietrofesa, 1970, p. 3).

Within more recent times, the American Personnel and Guidance Association (APGA) has given increased attention to counseling and to the professionalization of counseling. Additionally, state departments of education have adopted standards for counseling and all of the fifty states have enacted laws pertaining to certification for school counselors.

The mid 1970s witnessed several moves to pass laws providing for licensure of counselors in private practice. In 1975, Virginia became the first state to pass such a law. The American Personnel and Guidance Association has taken an active interest in counselor licensure legislation and reports that in 1976-77 licensure laws were being considered in twenty-one states (Van Hoose and Kottler, 1977, p. 124).

Counseling Defined Counseling is a professional service performed by professionally trained counselors. It is not a casual encounter designed to "adjust" or "straighten out" the client. Counseling is a process designed to accelerate the growth of the client.

Rogers' (1952) definition of counseling is as follows:

> The process by which the structure of the self is relaxed in the safety of the relationship with the therapist, and previously denied experiences are perceived and then integrated into an altered self. [p. 70]

Tyler (1969) in a summary statement notes that "the purpose of counseling is to facilitate wise choices of the sort on which the person's later development depends" (p. 13). She makes cognizant the fact that counseling is developmental as well as adjustive in nature. Counseling can be helpful to all individuals since choices are made throughout the life span. Maximum developmental potentials become more realistic attainments through the counseling endeavor. Stefflre (1970) goes one step further in his view of counseling. He states:

> Counseling denotes a professional relationship . . . designed to help the client understand and clarify his view of

his life space so that he may make meaningful and informed choices consonant with his essential nature and his particular circumstances . . .

Counseling is a learning-teaching process, for the client learns about his life space . . . If he is to make meaningful and informed choices, he must know himself, the facts of his present situation, and the possibilities . . . as well as the most likely consequences of the various choices . . . [pp. 252-253]

So counseling concerns center on choice and decision-making processes regarding (1) self, (2) others, and (3) environmental influences. While Stefflre does say that counseling is a "teaching-learning process," he is primarily emphasizing it as one part of a process which could range on a continuum from teaching all the way to psychotherapy. He continues, "But counseling differs from teaching in that its goals are more determined by the individual and less by society . . ." (p. 253).

The relationship between client and counselor is generally viewed as a most important element in the process. Kell and Mueller (1966) discuss some dimensions of this relationship:

The complexities, subtleties, and intensity of a counseling relationship increase dramatically as the relationship becomes more meaningful to its participants. The increasing significance of the relationship is the key to its therapeutic value. [p. 20]

Many definitions of counseling also stress specific functions of the counselor in the counseling process. Wrenn (1962), for example, writes that the counselor aids students in self-understanding and self-acceptance and emphasizes the need for the counselor to be sensitive to cultural changes that affect student self-understanding. Wrenn (1970) more recently reiterated this position:

A large emphasis of modern counselors in any setting is to aid in the process of self-identification, in helping a person answer the questions of 'Who am I and what am I here for?' Counselors are both good listeners who provide for emotional catharsis and gradual self-enlightenment upon the part of the client, and they serve as resources of information

> about the vocational and social world of the client's present and his projected future. A counselor aids in decision-making, in expanding his client's range of alternatives or options open to him, in modifying his behavior patterns in desired directions. [p. 33]

Counseling, furthermore, becomes a way of life for the counselor, and is not turned on or turned off like the kitchen faucet. A counselor acts in a facilitative manner—and in contrast to what some may think—a manner which is unpredictable, since it is authentic and not contrived. But a counselor also tries to approach people with some consistency. He/She basically believes in human beings and their worth and dignity.

Essentially, the authors of this volume believe that counseling can be described as *the process through which a person professionally prepared to counsel attempts to help another person in matters of self-understanding, decision making, and problem solving.* Counseling is a face-to-face human encounter and its outcome is greatly dependent upon the quality of the counseling relationship.

The Goals of Counseling The professional counselor needs to seek answers to such questions as "What does the client expect from counseling?" and "Does counseling do any good?" To answer these questions, he/she must consider client expectations and needs as well as his/her own goals for counseling. Thus, counseling goals derive from two major services. One of these is the counselor's own theory and philosophy of counseling. The way the counselor views counseling, his/her value system, and beliefs about humanness will determine in large measure the goals for counseling. Put another way, the professional counselor has some general goals which give direction to his/her work with clients. Ultimately, however, counseling goals must be formulated in terms applicable to the life situation of a particular client.

The second source of goals derive form the client's needs and expectations. Arbuckle (1965) writes:

> It is likely that the goals and objectives expressed by individuals for other people are reflective rather of the needs of the person who expresses the goal than of the people for whom we supposedly have the goal. [pp. 50-51]

The counselor must first consider client needs and client satisfaction, and not counselor satisfaction. The important consideration is not what the client decides to do but whether this decision is best for the client (Arbuckle, 1965, p. 51).

The general goals which the counselor formulates as a result of a personal and professional philosophy will serve as a basis for the formulation of specific goals as the counselor works with a particular client. Blocher (1966) supports this position when he states that both client and counselor are directly involved in determining the specific goals for counseling (p. 157).

Counselor Goals Counseling has often been criticized for a lack of clearly defined or instrumental goals. Arbuckle (1965) has made some particularly sharp comments regarding the posture of counselors. He writes:

> Far too many counselors do not know *what* they are doing, but an even larger number do not appear to have a very good understanding of *why* they are doing what they are doing, or *what* they think they are doing. Thus we have counselors who know what they are doing, but do not know why they are doing it; we have others who know why they should be doing something, but not how to do it. [pp. 49-50]

Setting clearly defined goals is indeed difficult, but it is crucial for establishing direction in counseling. Hill (1975) states, "Few clients come to the counselor with clearly defined problems; in fact, even after extensive self-exploration and the establishment of . . . understanding, a client's self-expression often remains global, vague, and ambiguous" (p. 571). She goes on to note that too often, even upon termination, neither counselor nor client has an idea of whether or not intervention was facilitative.

The behaviorists in particular see many of the traditional goals of counseling as too vague and general to be helpful. Krumboltz (1966) argues that the goals of counseling will be more useful if stated in terms of specific behaviors rather than in such broadly defined terms as "self-understanding" and "self-acceptance." First, he defines the criteria for a set of goals. They are as follows:

1. The goals of counseling should be capable of being stated differently for each individual client.
2. The goals of counseling should be compatible with, though not necessarily identical to, the values of the counselor.
3. The degree to which the goals of counseling are attained by each client should be observable. [p. 155]

He goes on to suggest three categories under which numerous specific goals can be listed. His goal categories are: (1) Altering Maladaptive Behavior, (2) Learning the Decision-Making Process, and (3) Preventing Problems.

Patterson (1970) points out that part of the problem with counseling goals is that there appears to be several levels of objectives, or differences in specificity or generality. He talks about the goals of counseling as *ultimate, mediate,* and *immediate.* Patterson's *ultimate* goal is "self-actualization," "self-realization," or "self-enhancement." Essentially, it is a long-term outcome. He argues that the concept of "self-actualization" provides a "common or universal need or goal, not only of counseling and of all helping relationships, but of life. Counseling is thus consistent with life and its goal is not something apart from everyday living, but inherent in it" (Patterson, 1970, p. 176).

The *mediate* goals of Patterson (1970) are the more specific goals or subgoals of counseling which attempt to develop individual potential. While the ultimate goal is common to all counseling, the mediate goals may vary among individuals. The *immediate* goal of counseling is to set in motion, and continue, a process of intrapersonal exploration which will lead to the mediate and ultimate goals sought. Elsewhere, Patterson (1969) goes on to say:

> Self-exploration perhaps consists of several aspects or stages. Before an individual can engage in intrapersonal exploration he must be able to reveal or expose himself. Thus, the first step is self-disclosure. Self-exploration, perhaps beginning with negative aspects of the self followed by more positive aspects, can then occur. The later stages of the process lead to increasing self-awareness, which makes possible the development of the characteristics of the fully functioning person ... [p. 16]

Essentially, then, the goals of counseling become self-exploration, self-understanding, and action. Ponzo (1976) suggests three interrelated phases consisting of awareness, cognitive reorganization, and behavior change. It is within this framework that client and counselor formulate individualized goals for the client.

Hackney and Nye (1973) stress the desirability of mutual goal setting. As the counselor begins to understand why the client came for counseling, he/she then begins to help the client explore troublesome behaviors and feelings. The counselor and client then begin formulating goals together that are directly related to the client's needs and problems (p. 40).

Client Expectations The counselor has goals or objectives that he/she hopes can be achieved through counseling. Generally the goals have a philosophical base and, with modification, are applicable to the counselor's work with all clients. On the other hand, clients have expectations for counseling. Individuals who seek assistance expect counseling to answer questions, produce solutions, or relieve stressful situations. All too often clients expect counseling to point them in the right direction and solve their problems. Shertzer and Stone (1968) write that the client "usually expects to be tested, analyzed, and above all told what to do to obtain whatever it was that led him to counseling" (p. 96).

There is some research dealing rather specifically with what individuals and certain groups expect from counseling. Perrone, Weiking, and Nagel (1965) asked junior high school students and their parents and teachers to express their views on counseling. These researchers sought to determine whether the three groups differed in their recommendations for counseling for students with many problems and students with few problems as measured by the Mooney Problem Checklist. Significant differences were reported between parents and students and parents and teachers, but no significant differences were found between students and teachers. However, Perrone, Weiking, and Nagel suggested that parents seemed to be more in favor of intensive counseling than either students or teachers. In fact, teachers placed the least value on counseling. Students with few problems recommended counseling for "queer" students. Students with many problems suggested counseling for "homely" types.

Dunlop (1965) sought to determine the attitudes of counselors, counselor educators, school administrators, parents, and high school seniors, to the appropriateness of certain counselor functions. He found that all of the above groups had positive attitudes toward counseling which dealt with educational and vocational planning. He concluded that most parents and students expect counselors to serve as advice givers.

Other surveys suggest that parents and teachers expect counselors to help students select a college, find a vocation, and improve school performance. Some adults want counselors to help students do the "right" thing or make the "best" choice or, to put it bluntly, to do what adults want done. They do not view counseling as particularly necessary in dealing with personal or emotional problems, nor do they see counseling as a service which helps students make long-range plans leading to personal effectiveness and happiness.

Many professional counselors would consider the above expectations inappropriate and ill-conceived. Nevertheless, there is often a clear discrepancy between what counselors view as appropriate goals and the expectations of their clients.

Counselor Goals and Client Expectations: A Synthesis Such ultimate goals of counseling as "self-actualization," "self-acceptance," and "self-understanding" are helpful in that they provide a concept and a frame of reference for the counselor. Presumably counselors and all members of the helping profession want their clients to become "self-accepting" and "self-actualized" people. So the problem is not with these ultimate goals. The problem lies in agreeing upon short-range goals or stepping-stones leading eventually to the ultimate goal of self-actualization. We can agree with Patterson (1970) that general or ultimate goals may be appropriate for all clients. The more immediate and specific goals may apply only to some counselees.

On the question of who selects the goals for counseling, it is our position that the professional counselor, possessing some depth of knowledge of human growth and development, should be alert to the needs of his/her clients and further should know the purposes of the counselor's job. He/she is thus directly involved in goal setting and takes cues from the developmental status and present need of his/her clients.

This means that the specific goals for counseling adolescents in a Job Corps Center may be considerably different from specific goals for counseling in an elementary school. Blocher (1966) speaks to this point in his admirable statement on the formulation of counseling goals. He believes that effective counseling takes place only when goals are based upon specific and immediately perceived needs in the life situation of clients (p. 158). Hosford (1969) clarifies this even further when he states:

> It is important, however, that the goals of the counselor be relevant to those of the client. Unless counselors work with their clients in developing goals which communicate specifically what the client will be able to do when the counseling is terminated, there may be times in which the outcome of counseling will have little relationship to the problem for which the individual sought help . . . [p. 6]

An example of counseling based upon specific client needs is seen in this excerpt from a tape recording of an interview with an adolescent male.

Counselor: I got the note from Miss——saying that you wanted to see me right away.
Client: Yes, I was here this morning, but you were in a meeting or something. [*Pause*] Uh . . .
Counselor: Sorry I missed you, but we can have some time now.
Client: Well . . ., [*some hesitation*] well, my dad and I, we, we, are fighting again. [*Pause*]
Counselor: The same old problem, huh?
Client: Yeah. He got up at 4 o'clock to go to work and he came and jacked me out of bed cussing and saying how lazy I was. And I had worked 'til 8 o'clock.
Counselor: So you had another fight.
Client: He slapped me, then he kicked me and I ran across the street . . .
Counselor: You ran out of the house.

> Client: ... and he came after me while I was on the neighbor's steps. They were icy and slick and I fell and hurt my ribs bad. And he says not to come back; and I'm not going back there; I'll never go back there [*crying*]. [*Pause*]
>
> Counselor: Once you said you may go live with your uncle.
>
> Client: Yeah ... I can't go back there ... I'd kill him if he wasn't my dad. [*Pause*] I can't go back ... I don't know what I'll do now ...
>
> Counselor: Maybe we can work out something ... uh, we gotta figure out what we can do now. If you can't go back home, you'll have to have some other place to stay.

The counselor, then, must be able to deal with some immediate concerns based upon the life situation of his clients. He/She needs also to be aware of the persisting needs of children and youth and to conceptualize his/her counseling goals accordingly. The following list of goals, while not exhaustive, is appropriate for counseling in schools. The counselor should seek to aid his/her clients in solving the developmental tasks of life with specific attention to assisting clients in the following areas:

1. Self-understanding and self-acceptance.
2. Attaining appropriate academic competency.
3. Dealing with personal and emotional problems.
4. Developing a method for realistic decision making.
5. Learning to deal with complex interpersonal relationships.
6. Aiding in vocational development.

We assume that the counselor makes tentative judgments about each client at the onset of counseling, and that he/she structures goals accordingly. The counselor may also need to readjust his/her goals when new insights are gained as a result of counseling.

The Process of Counseling Tyler (1969) writes that the aim of the helping process is to enable the client to cope with life. She believes that one outcome to be expected from counseling is that the client take some constructive action in his/her own behalf. Stefflre (1970) described counseling as a teaching-learning process carried on for the purpose of helping the counselee learn about him/herself. Blocher (1966) believes that counseling should aim at facilitating human learning of a deeply personal nature. He also describes counseling as "a planned, systematic intervention in the life of another human being. This intervention is aimed at changing that person's behavior" (p. 12).

Most counselors describe themselves as "helpers" or helping professionals, implying that at some point in the counseling process the help which they provide will be useful to the counselee and that it will be provided in a professional manner. Counselors attempt to help counselees resolve concerns, make decisions, and plan their future. Further, as Eisenberg and Delaney (1977) note, the "helping process also includes an exploration of the counselee's feelings and perceptions about self, significant others, and important aspects of his or her environment" (p. 3).

For purposes of our discussion, the counseling process will be defined as a systematic procedure in which the counselor intervenes in the life of another person for the purpose of helping that person change his/her behavior. Intervention follows mutual agreement of the counselor and client and is predicated upon the assumption that more adequate functioning or better adjustment will result from the intervention.

The crucial question of what actually happens in the counseling process to bring about change in the client has not yet been satisfactorily answered. It appears, however, that some aspects of the counseling process are universal. This is client exploration of self or intrapersonal exploration (Patterson, 1970). Rogers (1951) speaks of movement in the type of verbal content presented by the client. He notes that initially clients tend to talk about symptoms and problems for a majority of the time. Later this type of talk tends to be replaced by statements about the self and about current behavior. Still later there tends to be an increase in client discussion of new actions in accord with the client's new understanding of the situation.

Client self-exploration and self-disclosure leading to insight is influenced by several aspects of the helping process. The conditions for effective interpersonal facilitating relationships are treated in later chapters. However, it is appropriate to point out here that several counselor behaviors during the interview will directly affect the ability and the willingness of the client to attempt self-exploration. Our experiences in counseling lead us to suggest that clients tend to deal with safe topics until they feel secure with the counselor. Further, there is a tendency for clients to deal initially with content topics rather than with affective matters or concerns. Understanding, openness, competence, and authenticity are the counselor's keys to helping clients move from a focus on the cognitive to a focus on the affective, and from a discussion of external matters to a discussion of self.

The following excerpt from a tape recorded first interview with a ninth-grade female illustrates this point.

> Counselor: Can you tell me a little about yourself?
> Client: There is not much to tell. [*Laughs nervously*]
> Counselor: Well, maybe you could just tell me anything that's on your mind. Uh ... anything you would like to talk about.
> Client: Like school, and things like that?
> Counselor: Like school, if you want, uh, and about you. [*Pause*]
> Client: Oh, school is all right. I get along O.K., only, uh, only me and Mr. ⎯⎯ aren't hitting it off too good.
> Counselor: I see.
> Client: Well, a lot of the other kids there, you know, they cause some trouble and I go along.

(Here the client gave a long description of the behavior of other students, in and out of school, with only brief references to herself. The first interview ended with a discussion of some problems of the client's friends.)

The second interview with the same client took place five days later. The following excerpts are from conversations in the last few minutes of the interview.

> Client: Uh, I'm kinda nervous. . . . I've never talked with anyone, er, a teacher or anybody like that, like this before.

Counselor: I'm glad you feel free to talk with me J——. [*Pause*] Sometimes it is hard to talk, but this is your time and I'm glad to help if I can.
Client: I don't know, I'm just mixed up I guess. [*Pause*]
Counselor: You just feel confused and mixed up.
Client: Sometimes I feel like I'm not me, you know, like I'm doing things and saying something that I know is wrong and bad, but I do it just the same.
Counselor: You don't know why you do or say some things.
Client: Oh, I know what I'm doing, but I don't care sometimes I guess. Then after I wish I hadn't. And I think about it, I think about it a lot. After, I always do. [*Pause*] But then it's too late.
Counselor: And then you feel bad.
Client: Yeah, bad.

Effective counseling, then, requires movement from symptoms to self, from a focus on the environment and others to a focus upon the self. Both the quality and quantity of this process are influenced by the client's perceptions and feelings about the helping situation.

As briefly noted above, another type of change that occurs in counseling involves an affective component. Kell and Mueller (1966) believe that as the client develops insight he/she switches from a cognitive to an affective or affective-intellectual dimension. They write:

> Both affective and cognitive dimensions enter into an effective counseling process. However, we wish also to emphasize that we think it is rare that significant changes in human behavior occur without an effective experience. Change in behavior in regard to other humans, the interpersonal dimension, as we understand it, almost invariably calls for an affective, and often, conflicted experience. [p. 85]

Rogers (1951) states that during the process of counseling, clients tend to move also from a consideration of the past to a focus on the present. In the consideration of any conflict or problem, especially if it is threatening or painful, the client tends to begin with some past aspect and only gradually begins to face the more crucial and often unpleasant issue as it exists in the present. The client gradually learns to leave the less dangerous consideration of symptoms—others, the environment, and the past—and begins to focus upon "me," "here," and "now" (Rogers, 1951, pp. 135-136).

The counseling process can be further described as a continuous process of interaction between counselor and client. The process begins at the time of agreement of counselor and counselee to enter into such a relationship. As Blocher (1966) describes it, this "contract" between client and counselor is the beginning point in counseling. The agreement or contract can be expected to grow and change as the client's perceptions of his/her needs grow and change. The agreement can be terminated when the client's situation is altered sufficiently to permit independence from the relationship.

SUMMARY

The purpose of this chapter has been to provide an overview of counseling and the counseling process. Our attention has focused primarily upon a conceptual consideration of counseling with specific attention to in-counseling behavior of counselors. We do not intend to simply provide a how-to-do-it kit or a guide for effective counseling practice. We have not attempted to sell an approach or to emphasize any particular "school" of counseling. In this chapter, and in those that follow, we plan to demonstrate our conviction that the professional counselor requires a frame of reference encompassing not only a theoretical position on humanness, but also an understanding of how the self of the counselor influences counseling relationships and counseling outcomes.

REFERENCES

Arbuckle, Dugald S.
   1965 *Counseling: Philosophy, Practice and Theory.* Boston: Allyn and Bacon.

Aubrey, R.F.
   1977 "Historical Development of Guidance and Counseling and Implications for the Future." *Personnel and Guidance Journal,* 55(6), 288–295.

Blocher, Donald H.
   1966 *Developmental Counseling.* New York: The Ronald Press.

Darley, J. G.
   1937 "Tested Maladjustment Related to Clinically Diagnosed Maladjustment." *Journal of Applied Psychology,* 21:632-642.

Dunlop, Richard H.
1965 "Professional Educators, Parents, and Students Assess the Counselor's Role." *Personnel and Guidance Journal.* 43:1024-1028. Reprinted with permission of the publisher, American Personnel and Guidance Association, Washington, D.C.

Eisenberg, S., and Delaney, D. J.
1977 *The Counseling Process,* 2nd Ed. Chicago. Rand McNally.

Hackney, H., and Nye, S.
1973 *Counseling Strategies and Objectives,* Englewood Cliffs, N.J.: Prentice Hall Inc.

Hill, C.
1975 "A Process Approach for Establishing Counseling Goals and Outcomes." *Personnel and Guidance Journal,* 53(8), 571-576.

Hosford, Ray E.
1969 "Behavioral Counseling—A Contemporary Overview." *The Counseling Psychologist,* 1:1-32.

Kell, Bill L., and Mueller, William T.
1966 *Impact and Change: A Study of Counseling Relationships.* New York: Appleton-Century-Crofts, Educational Division, Meredith Corporation.

Krumboltz, John D.
1966 "Behavioral Goals for Counseling." *Journal of Counseling Psychology,* 13:153-159.

Patterson, C. H.
1969 "A Current View of Client-Centered or Relationship Therapy." *The Counseling Psychologist,* 1:2-24.

1970 "A Model for Counseling and Other Facilitative Human Relationships." In W. Van Hoose, and J. Pietrofesa, eds. *Counseling and Guidance in the Twentieth Century.* Boston: Houghton Mifflin, pp. 173-188.

Perrone, P., Weiking, M. L., and Nagel, E. H.
1965 "The Counseling Function as Seen by Students, Parents, and Teachers." *Journal of Counseling Psychology,* 12:148-152.

Ponzo, Z.
1976 "Integrating Techniques from Five Counseling Theories." *Personnel and Guidance Journal,* 54(8), 414-419.

Rogers, Carl R.
1942 *Counseling and Psychotherapy.* Boston: Houghton Mifflin.

1951 *Client-Centered Therapy.* Boston: Houghton Mifflin.

1952 "Client-Centered Psychotherapy." *Scientific American,* 187:66-74.

Shertzer, Bruce, and Stone, Shelley C.
1968 *Fundamentals of Counseling.* Boston: Houghton Mifflin.

Stefflre, Buford.
1970 "Counseling in the Total Society: A Primer." In W. Van Hoose, and J. Pietrofesa, eds. *Counseling and Guidance in the Twentieth Century.* Boston: Houghton Mifflin, pp. 251-265.

Tyler, Leona.
   1969 *The Work of the Counselor.* New York: Appleton-Century-Crofts, Educational Division, Meredith Corporation.

Van Hoose, W., and Kottler, J.
   1977 *Ethical and Legal Issues in Counseling and Psychotherapy.* San Francisco: Jossey-Bass Inc.

Van Hoose, William H., and Pietrofesa, John J.
   1970 *Counseling and Guidance in the Twentieth Century.* Boston: Houghton Mifflin.

Williamson, E. G.
   1939 *How to Counsel Students: A Manual of Techniques for Clinical Counselors.* New York: McGraw-Hill.

Wrenn, C. Gilbert.
   1962 *The Counselor in a Changing World.* Washington, D.C.: American Personnel and Guidance Association.
   1970 "The World of the Counselor . . . and You." *Cadence,* 1:32-36.

Chapter 2 Focusing on Growth

INTRODUCTION It is the viewpoint of the authors that counseling is a learning process and that it can be successful only to the degree that learning takes place. A basic consideration, then, must be what one hopes to accomplish through counseling. As stated previously, ultimate goals would seem to be the development of a healthy, mature, self-actualizing person in the sense that Maslow (1962) has described. Consequently, it is the task of the counselor to create the conditions that will make it possible for growth and progress to occur. He/She must help the client to grow in decision-making capacity without predetermining which direction the client should take.

Let us be very clear. Until and unless a relationship is established between counselor and client, little or no growth can take place. Once this relationship is established, the client can be helped to progress through the counseling process in the following fashion:

1. Establishment of relationship
2. Gaining of insight
3. Examination of alternatives
4. Decision making

Recent research has demonstrated that certain attitudes, processes, and conditions can influence the growth of the client. Noteworthy in this regard has been the work of Truax and Carkhuff (1967) in the past several years. They have accumulated an impressive body of data that indicates the importance of five "facilitative conditions" (pp. 80-143). These are concreteness, warmth (nonpossessive), accurate empathy, genuineness, and degree of intensity/intimacy. The presence of high levels of these conditions seems to be closely related to client growth and low levels of these conditions are related to no growth or regression. As Truax and Carkhuff (1967) conclude:

> Counseling research findings suggest that the human encounter itself, even when intended to be facilitative or helpful can be for better or for worse, whether we are focusing on changes in personality functioning, changes in verbal condition, changes in social development, changes in the learning of arithmetic, or changes in college academic achievements. [p. 143]

Learning, of course, is a personal experience and we as counselors cannot force our perceptions upon those of the client—*even if we try.* Many counselors mistakenly feel they can use their own opinions to change their clients' behavior. This is impossible. Even though the client may superficially agree with suggestions made in the course of the interview, he/she will seldom follow through unless he/she is personally convinced of the import of their meaning. Learning and self-discovery must come from within.

In order to help the counselee grow, the counselor needs to focus upon certain dimensions of that individual. Does he/she concern him/herself with observable behavior? Should he/she concentrate upon counselee feelings and attitudes? To do either, or perhaps both, the counselor needs a psychological conception of humanness. While some counselors deny they hold such a conception and some counselors may feel that it is unnecessary, we tend to believe that all counselors, although they may not be able to verbalize, do reflect in their dealings with others a psychological (and philosophical) model of humanness. Combs et al. (1969) saw the perceptions of the helping person as crucial if he/she is to be effective. Concurrently, the counselor will find of crucial importance the perceptions of the counselee in order to affect precipitant or resultant behavioral change.

SOME PSYCHOLOGICAL CONSIDERATIONS OF SELF-DEVELOPMENT
The self-concept, a hypothetical construct encompassing all of the values, attitudes, and beliefs toward one's self in relation to the environment, is a composite of numerous self-percepts which influence and to a great degree determine perception and behavior (Pietrofesa, 1969). Anderson (1965) says that, "Everyone has an image or a concept of himself as a unique person or self, different from every other self. This concept pertains to one's self both as a physical person and as a psychological person—i.e., each one has a physical self-image and psychological self-image" (p. 2). Research has tended to support the idea that self-concept is of great importance, but its essence has been captured best in a recent parable entitled "The Man Who Was Put in a Cage" (May, 1967). May describes a situation where a king decided to place in a cell a subject whose behaviors were to be observed by a psychologist. Following is the segment which describes the aforementioned "man" in the stage just prior to insanity:

> But when the king was not in the yard and the man was not aware that the psychologist was present, his expression was quite different—sullen and morose. When his food was handed to him through the bars by the keeper, the man would often drop the dishes or dump over the water and then would be embarrassed because of his stupidity and clumsiness. His conversation became increasingly one-tracked; and instead of the involved philosophical theories about the value of being taken care of, he had gotten down to simple sentences such as 'It is fate,' which he would say over and over again ... The psychologist was surprised to find that the man should be so clumsy ... or so stupid ... for he knew from his tests that the man had originally been of good average intelligence. Then it dawned upon the psychologist that this was the kind of behavior he had observed in some anthropological studies among the

Negroes in the South—people who had been forced to kiss the hand that fed and enslaved them, who could no longer hate or rebel. The man in the cage took more and more to simply sitting all day long in the sun as it came through the bars, his only movement being to shift his position from time to time from morning through the afternoon. [p. 162]

To fully understand the self-concept we must break it down into various components. (See Figure 1)

The Self as Seen by Self One major part of the self-concept is how the person sees him/herself. Is the individual seen as mature, sensitive, responsible and self-directing? This percept would certainly affect the individual's behavior. The underachiever, for example, sees him/herself as less adequate and so behaves accordingly (Frazier and Combs, 1958; Lowther, 1963; Snyder, 1966; Combs, 1964). Additionally, an individual with high self-esteem seeks a job with which there is equally high prestige (Korman, 1967) while a person with a negative self-perception is more likely to make an inadequate vocational choice (Patterson, 1957; Chambers and Lieberman, 1965).

The Self as Thought to be Seen by Others Each individual also develops attitudes as to how other people view him/herself and then tends to live up to these perceived expectations. The youth who feels his/her peers see him/her as "tough" will try to perform in that fashion. Carter (1968) suggests that the negative self-image of many Mexican-Americans is in reality a stereotype projected onto them which they adopt and consequently come to believe in themselves. The accuracy of adolescent self-perception and the reality of parental perceptions of their children are also related to the personal adjustment of those youngsters (McDaniels, 1968). A meaningful (though somewhat controversial) study concluded that perceiving children as superior achievers, and treating them as if they were, resulted in their behaving in that fashion (Rosenthal and Jacobson, 1968).

The counselor must be constantly aware of the premise that the amount of discrepancy between ideal self and perceived self is a noteworthy measure of adjustment. Consequently, the counselor must focus on—and gain an understanding of—both aspects in order to truly understand and help a client. Perhaps a good measure of counseling

Focusing on Growth 23

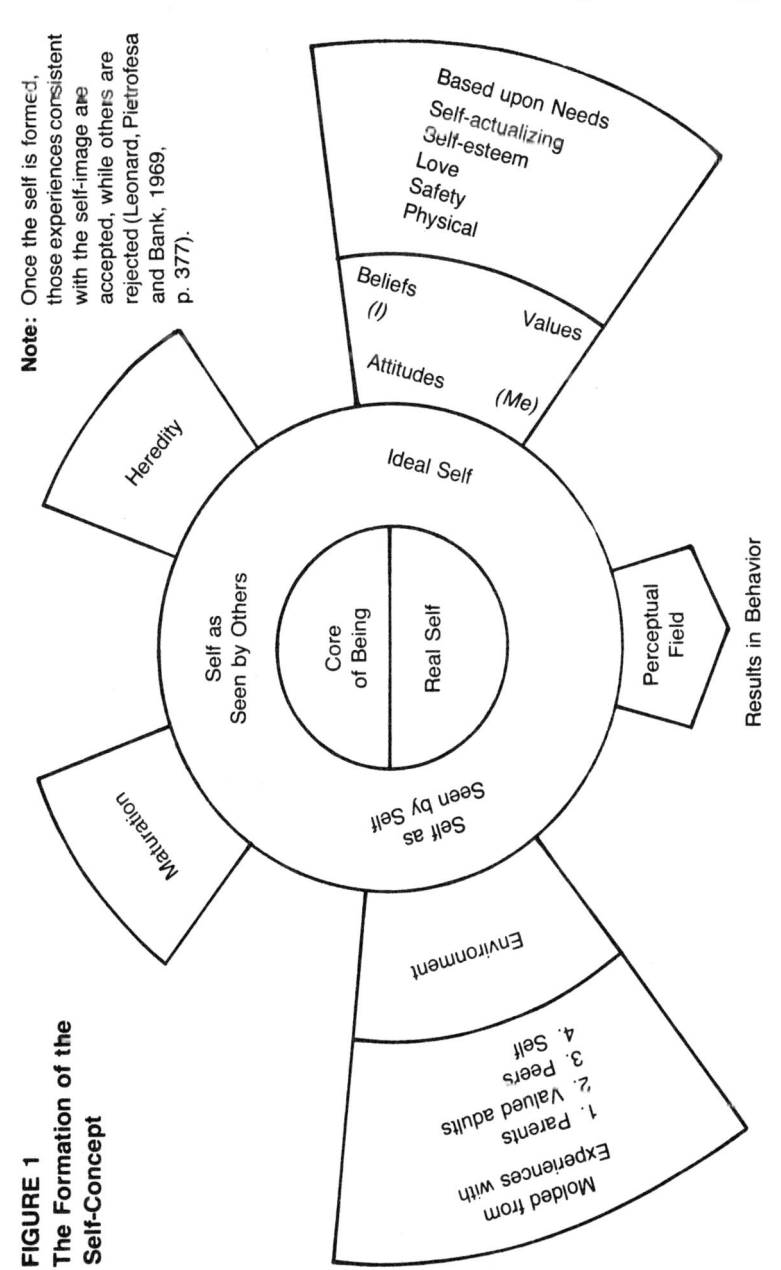

FIGURE 1
The Formation of the Self-Concept

Note: Once the self is formed, those experiences consistent with the self-image are accepted, while others are rejected (Leonard, Pietrofesa and Bank, 1969, p. 377).

- Based upon Needs
- Self-actualizing
- Self-esteem
- Love
- Safety
- Physical

Beliefs (I)
Values
Attitudes (Me)
Ideal Self

Heredity

Self as Seen by Others | Core of Being | Real Self
Self as Seen by Self

Perceptual Field

Results in Behavior

Maturation

Environment

Molded from Experiences with
1. Parents
2. Valued adults
3. Peers
4. Self

effectiveness is the extent to which a counselor can aid a client to reduce this discrepancy.

The Ideal Self   The ideal self represents the person one would like to become. Certain aspirations and goals are held dear. Havighurst et al. (1965) report that, "There is a great deal of evidence that the ideal self is deeply influenced by association with people who are in positions of prestige because they are older, more powerful, and better able to get the desirable things of life than the child or adolescent who observes them" (p. 238). The importance of this component of the self can be found in the fact that one does not generally become what one does not aspire to become. In order to develop into a good mechanic, you must see yourself as able to become a good mechanic. Established goals should be within reach, for otherwise the resulting frustrations and anxieties may do excessive damage to the self.

Dynamics of the Various Self-Percepts   The self-percepts of the healthy person are largely compatible and result in an individual who is comfortable with him/herself. This could be contrasted with a situation of divergent percepts which lead to conflict and nonhealth. Simplistically, Figure 2 illustrates this. Such a conflict might be found within juveniles who see themselves as being kind persons at heart but in order to maintain status in the eyes of peers resort to aggressive behavior. Similarly one might find conflict within young adults, who, while working at menial tasks, have rather high aspirational levels.

Reinforcement of the Self-Concept   As the individual grows older, the concept of self he/she has developed tends to become self-perpetuating. Humans need to order the world and, necessarily, perceive and behave in a fashion designed to bring about such order. This holds true regarding self-concept—that is, the individual uses selective perception (e.g., sees what one wants to see) and at times certain defensive postures (e.g., mechanisms that distort reality) to bring about consistency in one's views about oneself and the environment.

> While still in the process of making new discoveries concerning his properties as an individual, the growing child has a strong tendency to preserve ideas and attitudes he already has formed. He strives in the presence of others

FIGURE 2
Percepts Relationship

Unhealthy Mode

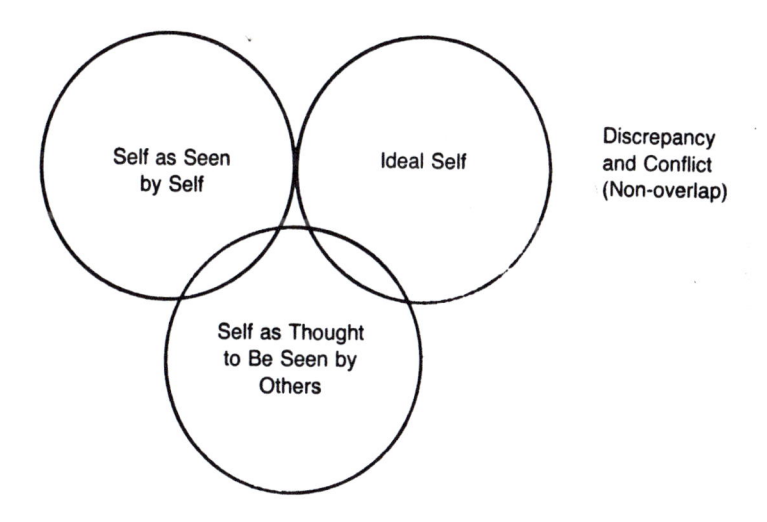

Discrepancy
and Conflict
(Non-overlap)

- Self as Seen by Self
- Ideal Self
- Self as Thought to Be Seen by Others

Healthy Mode

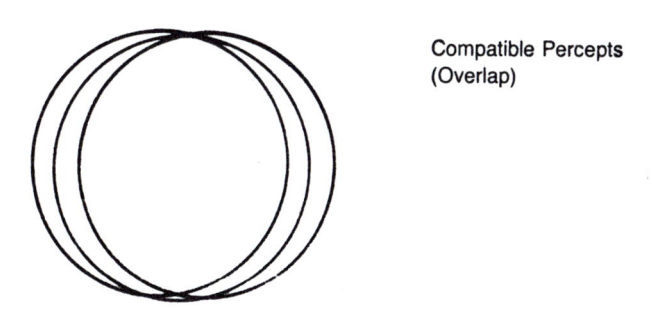

Compatible Percepts
(Overlap)

and in his own eyes to be himself (as he sees himself) and to live in accordance with his concepts or attitudes regarding himself, whether these be true or false.... He is likely to resist anything that is inconsistent with his own view of himself. It may even be difficult for him to hear or grasp the meaning of anything, favorable or unfavorable, that goes counter to his picture of himself. [Jersild, 1965, p. 205]

Children who see themselves as smart will behave in that fashion, will select those occurrences which substantiate that belief, and will discard or distort any encounters which contradict that belief.

Development of the Self-Concept The self-concept develops out of interaction with a number of variables. Two such variables, interactions with people, and reactions from people, provide the bases of the self. Brooks (1963) states that the child appears upon the human scene without self; the self is a social product conceived and born in the process of social interaction. Foremost among influences are parents. They play the dominant role in the child's life when he/she is most open to experience and also most dependent on others. Merrill (1965) notes that the most important group of social interaction is the family, for it is here the child acquires first impressions of human conditions. The family maintains this prominent position into the adolescent years, although admittedly, it becomes progressively less influential. The peer group gains in importance during the middle childhood years and becomes a primary force between the ages of twelve to seventeen. Significant adults—counselors, teachers, relatives—also contribute to the formation of the self. We do not want to belabor the point, but the emphasis is upon *significant* adults, since the adult who means little to the individual will not influence his/her thinking or behavior.

By significant people is meant those persons who are important or who have significance to the child by reason of his sensing their ability to allay insecurity or to intensify it—to increase or to decrease his sense of helplessness, to promote or to diminish his sense of well being. [Anderson, 1965, p. 6]

Felker (1974) in summary states that, "The self-concept is a dynamic circular force in human lives. Every human is vitally influenced by those around him" (p. 6). Interaction with others indicates to the person that he/she is "competent or incompetent, good or bad, worthy or unworthy" (p. 6).

A second variable, the material and nonmaterialistic environment, affects development. Youth raised in a materialistic society will be affected by either the abundance or scarcity of worldly goods. Contrasting cultures will spawn need patterns in their populace which may be quite different and mutually incompatible. Nonmaterial influences consist of thoughts, ideas, and values; for example, thoughts on the value of human life or what is beauty. Different influences may result in similar types of overt behavior. The rebellious affluent youngster may not watch television because it is a symbol of the "decadent" middle class, while a less well-to-do counterpart does not watch television because he/she has none.

While a major proportion of the self-concept is formulated in early life and while self-perpetuating influences press for consistency, the self-concept can be changed throughout one's lifetime. Brooks (1963) feels that if self-image is born of social interaction, then it can be reborn of social interaction. However, this can be a lengthy process at times. The implications of this become rather clear for both counselor and teacher in attempting to improve self-concept. Essentially, what will be needed is the opportunity to experience one's self in a more positive manner. Initially the individual may resist change but eventually the self will move in the particular direction the more positive experiences hold forth.

The Influence of Needs Individuals have needs they have to satisfy so they can live contentedly and in a healthy manner. The more basic needs—the need for food or drink—must be satisfied at least minimally for survival. Need satisfaction or nonsatisfaction influence the development of self-concept. For example, one who finds it difficult to satisfy a need may as a result think less of him/herself. In addition, he/she will have little time to spend in satisfying higher level needs. Concurrently, self-concept development helps to shape the expression of needs. The healthy youth expresses a need for achievement which does not violate the rights of others, while the unhealthy youth may express it in ways which attack society and eventually become self-destructive.

As a human being matures, he/she generally establishes some type of need pattern and comes to value certain modes of behavior that will enhance his/her functioning as a human being. In fact, the importance of needs are such that if they are not satisfied, the individual becomes depressed and less healthy. An extreme illustration of this is the large number of persons who lost their wealth during the depression and subsequently committed suicide.

Simplistically, individuals have a hierarchy of needs. The various levels, ranging from lower to higher, are according to Maslow (1954, pp. 80-92):

> **1.** *Physical needs: These needs are most basic for survival, e.g., food, drink, sleep, and waste elimination. The need to reproduce the species falls into this category. (Note: within this society, sex needs are undoubtedly tinged by other needs, the need for love or even the need for achievement.) When these needs are not satisfied, they tend to dominate the organism.*
>
> All other needs may become simply nonexistent or be pushed into the background. Then the whole organism might be characterized by saying that it is hungry, for consciousness is almost completely preempted by hunger. All capacities are put into the service of satisfying hunger. Now the sensory receptors and effectors, and intelligence, memory, habits—all may be defined simply as hunger-gratifying tools. Human capacities that are not useful for this purpose lie dormant or are pushed into the background. [Gale, 1969, p. 101]
>
> **2.** *Safety needs: Safety needs come into play when one's life is threatened. Essentially, they are concerned with self-preservation.*
>
> Another indication of the child's need for safety is his preference for some kind of undisrupted routine or rhythm. He seems to want a predictable, orderly world. For instance, injustice, unfairness, or inconsistency in the parents seem to make a child feel anxious and unsafe. This attitude may be not so much because of the injustice per se or any particular pains involved, but rather because this treatment threatens to make the world look unreliable, or unsafe, or unpredictable. Young children seem to thrive better under a system that has at least a skeletal outline of rigidity, in which

there is a schedule of a kind, some sort of routine, something that can be counted upon, not only for the present, but also far into the future. [Maslow, 1954, p. 86]

Small children in a strange and unfamiliar place may feel that their safety is threatened. Such a reaction is evidenced in children when they cling to a parent upon meeting a stranger. Similar types of reactions can be observed, in the adult, but, of course, they are more complex. The adult attacked verbally may withdraw inward. It is important to remember that under threat the individual's perception narrows, because of its defensive posture, and he/she concentrates on the threatening stimuli. This behavior may or may not appear appropriate to an observer who is not experiencing the same situation.

3. *Love needs:* Each of us has a need to be loved by others, and as a consequence, is able to love others. The reception of insufficient love will distort physical, intellectual, emotional, and spiritual growth. "In our society," Maslow (1954) writes, "the thwarting of these needs is the most commonly found core in cases of maladjustment and more severe psychopathology" (p. 89).

4. *Esteem needs:* There are a variety of self-esteem needs including achievement, approval, nurturance, autonomy, affiliation, adequacy, and curiosity. The satisfaction of such needs is tied intimately with developing an attitude of self-worth in an affluent American society.

Satisfaction of the self-esteem need leads to feelings of self-confidence, worth, strength, capability, and adequacy, of being useful and necessary in the world. But thwarting of these needs produces feelings of inferiority, of weakness, and of helplessness. These feelings in turn give rise to either basic discouragement or else compensatory or neurotic trends. [Maslow, 1954, p. 91]

Lacking, then, a sense of self-worth, the individual views him/herself in a negative fashion, and in fact, his/her perceptions of the world reflect the same.

5. *Self-actualization needs:* The need for self-actualization is the need to become more fully functioning and to utilize one's capacities in a most efficient manner. The search for a meaningful existence is a reality. One becomes less concerned with oneself and more concerned with others. One is able to identify with large groups of people. Gale (1969) says, "Our human nature seems to be such that we actually function more smoothly and happily when we are active, arresting, challenged, excited, and stimulated" (p. 111). Self-actualization, it should be remembered, is both state and process and its successful attainment depends upon the situation in which one finds oneself. One might be self-actualizing on the job, but become less so at home in a troubled marital situation.

One point to remember is that more than one need may be in operation at a time and also that the individual moves up and down the "ladder" of needs. As a need is satisfied, one then tries to obtain success at the next higher level. A person who is fed, clothed, and safe from physical harm can become concerned with love and esteem needs. If functioning at a higher need level means that a lower need satisfaction is withdrawn, a person will generally descend the need hierarchy in order to satisfy the more basic need.

When individuals function at different need levels, they probably do not understand each other very well. A person most concerned with the attainment of an "A" in school will not understand someone who might be trying to escape from the school bully or another who is hungry and unable to concentrate because of the odors from the cafeteria.

Need gratification then, particularly childhood gratification, is essential to the formation of the self. It is a psychologically sound suggestion that frustration is one determiner of hostility and, conversely, that gratification prevents the formation of hostile impulses. If a child is denied love, he/she constantly craves and seeks that love. On the other hand, this is not to say all needs must be satisfied directly, or at once, for to function within a society some frustration tolerance must be developed. One may imagine that there are increasing degrees of healthy character formation, dependent upon the satisfaction of social need requirements.

IMPLICATIONS FOR THE COUNSELOR Springing forth from (1) self-concept and its percepts, (2) the human influences on self-development, (3) hereditary maturational, and environmental growth patterns, and (4) need patterns, comes the perceptual field which results in one's behavior. All of the preceding elements play a crucial role in counseling. Boyd (1970), for instance, found in two studies that the counselee's self-concept will determine the method of establishing rapport, means of motivating the counselee, and the counseling techniques utilized. She states that, "To bring about change the counselor has to have an understanding of the counselee's self-concept" (p. 307). One reason for presenting this elemental model is that it provides much in the way of allowing the counselor to focus upon growth of the counselee in a variety of fashions. The counselor can focus upon the needs of the individual or the self-concept or any of its percepts. The counselor can also focus upon peer or parental influences of past determinants of behavior. Although not a concern of this book, an elemental model provides a basis for consultative work with individuals in the counselee's environment. As a consequence, this model allows the counselor the possibility of looking at the counseling relationship in terms of immediate, mediate, and ultimate goals (Patterson, 1970) Specific behavioral change can be viewed as an immediate end, while counselee self-actualization and and authenticity become the ultimate goals. The counselor is capable of defining different goals for each counselee.

For example, the counselee or the counselor may feel that a negative self-concept is a crucial concern of this counselee. The joint enterprise becomes one of effecting positive movement in self-image. In order to work with self-concept the counselor must see how the client looks at him/herself and his/her experiences, and tells his/her experience. In addition, if the self-concept is to be changed, the mechanisms which maintain the concept should be understood. The counselor can provide a counseling situation in which the counselee can look at self-concept and its development, perceptual field, and resultant behaviors. In this instance, self-concept becomes the focus of the counselor who hopes to bring about change in behavior.

Self-theory would imply that counseling should (1) "encourage self-exploration" in clients, (2) provide continuous supportive counseling to foster positive self-concepts and, at the same time, accentuate individual strengths," and (3) help clients change the environment (Copeland, 1977, p. 399).

Thorne (1967) offers several implications for the Psychology of Integration from self-concept and ego structure determination.

1. The self-concept is a high-level general factor, the valence of which determines the valence of attitudes towards the self and others.

2. The composition of the self-concept determines the levels of performance and achievement to which the person aspires.

3. The person must like himself in order to have self-confidence and be able to face the world. However, some dissatisfaction with self-status may be a necessary precondition for change.

4. Important discrepancies between the actual and ideal self-statuses may result in anxiety, which ideally may stimulate compensatory efforts. Too great self-inconsistencies or discrepancies between actual and ideal selves may result in demoralization.

5. Higher-level integrations depend upon volitional consciousness, normal operation of controls, and intact executive self-functioning.

6. Mental health depends upon strong ego-functioning (p. 253).

The counselor could work in a reverse fashion by attempting to change behavior leading to a change in experiences and resulting in a change in self-concept. The behavioral change itself works in a curative fashion.

A Mexican-American secretary came to the counseling center with feelings of inadequacy founded in the belief that others did not like her, particularly her co-workers (secretaries) at the office. They had not talked to her and she, being rather shy, had not spoken to them since beginning work several weeks earlier. During counseling, she suggested as her first course of action the possibility of a party at her place to which all secretaries would be invited. The counselor pointed out that they might all decline the invitation at this stage. Gradually, the course of action most acceptable was that the counselee would say 'Hello' each morning for the next week to one secretary. The following week she would greet two secretaries and so forth. By the end of the fifth week the counselee was on a friendly basis with the office staff and was invited to a party at one of their homes.

In this case the counselor focused upon behavior change in the hope that it would have an eventual impact upon self-concept.

For certain clients the counselor cannot be passive. For example, Copeland (1977) emphasizes that, for Black women, insight approaches are insufficient. It is important to "produce" clients "willing to take control of their lives, who can cope with the environment, and who feel enough confidence within themselves to attempt to change the environment" (p. 400). The point to be made is that a counselor can promote growth in several ways. An excerpt from Lecky (1961) supports the contention that counseling may well provide the basis for a reexamination of self.

> Since each personality is an organized system in which every idea is related to every other, it is obvious that any attempt to force the issue and remove resistance by attacking it misses the point completely. For this reason the consultant will probably be more successful if he does not try too hard. Parents and teachers, whose own peace of mind is affected by the child's success or failure, usually cannot set aside their personal interest in the matter and are likely to become impatient. We may with advantage remind ourselves that only the individual himself can solve it his own way. [p. 298]

And finally, Rogers (1968) summarized that at the conclusion of counseling, the individual feels more comfortable with him/herself and experiences him/herself as more unified (p. 439).

THE FOCUS UPON SELF-ACTUALIZATION AND SELF-CONCEPT

The Self-Actualizing Person   If we accept the primary (ultimate) goal of counseling as the facilitation of the development of self-actualizing people capable of making their own decisions, we should describe such persons just briefly at this point. (See chapter 7). What, then is characteristic behavior for self-actualizing people? They must be able to see themselves as being liked and accepted by others. They must, more importantly, see themselves as being able to face the world with its concomitant problems and be able to make decisions that will be best not only for themselves but also for those around them, as being able and adequate to deal with life *not* because of what Horney (1937) has termed "the tyranny of the should," or because they are afraid *not* to do or accomplish, but because they *want* to accomplish certain aims and goals. This, admittedly, is ideal, but the conclusion is clear. It is important to focus on how the person sees him/herself because it will determine to a great degree whether a person is either adjusted or maladjusted, successful or unsuccessful. Individuals who can see themselves as unliked, unworthy, unable, and unimportant are those who fill our hospitals and/or jails. It is worthy of note that in recent years we have had the assassinations of John and Robert Kennedy and Martin Luther King. In each case these assassinations were perpetrated by individuals with negative self-perceptions. A major objective of the counseling process must be to aid the client in gaining a realistic, accepting perception of him/herself. Only in this fashion will growth take place that will affect behavior. Hardly less important is the need for the client to gain a realistic evaluation of others that is not affected by his/her own self-perceptions. And, finally, the need for an individual to become a real and authentic self is essential. Rogers (1958) stated:

> As I follow the experience of many clients in the therapeutic relationship which we endeavor to create for them, it seems to me that each one has the same problem. Below the level of the problem situation about which the individual is complaining—behind the trouble with studies, or wife, or employer, or with his own uncontrollable or bizarre behavior, or with his frightening feelings lies one central search. It seems to me that at bottom each person is asking: Who am I really? How can I get in touch with this real self, underlying

all my surface behavior? How can I become myself? ... it appears that the goal the individual most wishes to achieve, the end which he knowingly pursues, is to become himself. [pp. 9-10]

The Healthy Self-Conception as a Goal in Counseling The adequate healthy person has a more positive self-concept, learned from having been liked and from having been successful. The mature, healthy person also is one who can identify with others and is sensitive to their feelings and reactions in a particular situation. This, too, is learned. The adequate person, moreover, is one who can be near others, and yet not fear them because he/she is able to interact in an acceptable fashion with them. Such a person does not suffer from tunnel vision; he/she is able to think of others instead of thinking only of him/herself and of self-protection (Combs, 1962, p. 56). The counselor can help to increase the acceptance of the client by others by providing an atomsphere wherein he/she can discuss others as well as him/herself openly. Thus, the client will be aided to feel comfortable with his/her reactions to tohers and then transfer the attitudes to his/her behavior. Note how this is apparent in the following excerpt of an interview.

Counselor: How are things today, John?
Client: I just got the word that this is my absolute last chance to graduate. I just have to make it this time.
Counselor: The pressure is really on now, eh?
Client: It scares me—honest! I don't know if I'll be able to do it.
Counselor: Um-hum.
Client: I just have to make it—I've got the chance and it's up to me to take advantage of it ...
Counselor: You wonder if you can do it ...
Client: I know I can—it's just that I've been smacked down on my face so much by teachers that this makes me wonder if I can do it at times ...
Counselor: If only they'll give you a fair chance ...
Client: Yeah—just give me a chance to get back in the swing —which I can do ... I have done well

Counselor: before, but these damn unfair teachers—they think I'm a playboy and won't change their opinion of me—I can't take that . . .

Counselor: Not much future in operating that way.

Client: I guess they have reasons; I really haven't given them much of a chance either, maybe . . . I've been working on my math. She says I'm beginning to show progress and I know I'm going to make it there. I've been doing my homework the best that I could and she's been giving me a little bit of help every now and then, so I think I'll pass this term. It will be the first math class I've passed, so I'm keeping it up. And in English, there are so many dudes in that class that give her a hard time that she goes crazy, but why does she take it out on me?

Counselor: You're making progress but you're afraid she might spoil everything . . .

Client: Damn! I'm going to keep working at it. I'm going to try and get all caught up. There's this girl, see, who's helping me, especially in my writing. Even though old ⎯⎯ is not fair to me, she's been ok sometimes before. All I have to do is show her . . .

Counselor: It's all up to you . . .

Client: I feel a little bit of the old self-confidence coming back. Talking to you about this makes it seem so great, really!

    The growth of the client even in this short excerpt seems evident. In this regard it is worthy of note to state that openness to others and acceptance of them are also learned. Various studies (Combs, 1962) have found that handicapped persons can readily accept their handicaps if those around them accept them (p. 59). On the other hand, case studies of maladjusted, neurotic individuals show they reject others and are unable to deal with them in a healthy fashion. Thus, the counseling process must focus on helping an individual become more open to him/herself so he/she will then be able to be more open and accepting of others. In order for this to take place in counseling, the individual must be able to discover personal meaning in what is taking place in the counseling process, and must be simultaneously learning to meet his/her needs as well. This can lead to what could be termed a positive cycle in counseling as illustrated by the following schema (adapted from Combs, 1962, p. 185.) (See Figure 3).

In order for counseling to progress according to the positive cycle noted above, the counselor will often find it necessary to focus upon conflicts in needs or goals that clients are experiencing. These conflicts are readily seen as crucial in the adjustment of the individual. Making decisions covering these can be further seen as a necessary part of the growth process. In this regard, it may be helpful to review Cameron's (1947, pp. 133-134) classification of conflicts with examples of each:

1. *Approach-Avoidant:* The typical approach-avoidant conflict consists of two incompatible reactions arising in the same act or situation. An example would be a client's desire to attend a particular social event despite the fact that someone the client dislikes intensely will be there. An additional example would be a student wishing to take a particular course with an instructor whom he/she has had unhappy experiences.

FIGURE 3
The Positive Cycle of Client Growth Through Counseling

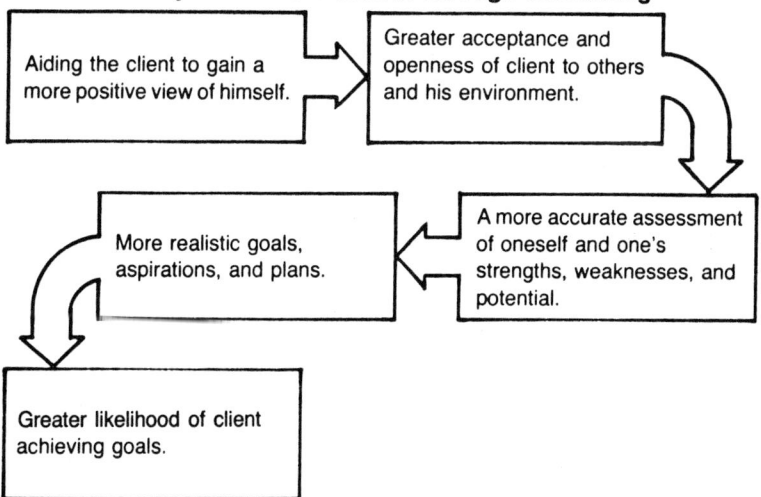

```
┌─────────────────────────┐   ┌─────────────────────────────┐
│ Aiding the client to    │──▶│ Greater acceptance and      │
│ gain a more positive    │   │ openness of client to others│
│ view of himself.        │   │ and his environment.        │
└─────────────────────────┘   └─────────────────────────────┘
                                            │
            ┌─────────────────────┐   ┌─────────────────────────────┐
            │ More realistic      │◀──│ A more accurate assessment  │
            │ goals, aspirations, │   │ of oneself and one's        │
            │ and plans.          │   │ strengths, weaknesses, and  │
            └─────────────────────┘   │ potential.                  │
                    │                 └─────────────────────────────┘
                    ▼
┌─────────────────────────┐
│ Greater likelihood of   │
│ client achieving goals. │
└─────────────────────────┘
```

2. *Approach-Approach:* The approach-approach conflict consists of "two incompatible reactions arising in the same act, both of which are directed toward different activities, objects or goals." An example of this is a parent's offering a child a present in exchange for giving up a desired activity or object.

3. *Avoidant-Avoidant:* The double avoidant conflict consists of "two incompatible reactions arising in the same act, each of which is directed away from an object, activity, or goal." The individual caught in such a situation cannot win and will get hurt no matter what the decision. Examples of this include the client who is threatened with pain or rejection if he/she does not go through with a disagreeable or humiliating situation, the person who has to apologize to another or be rejected, the adult who is trapped in a disagreeable job with no perceived alternative, and the student who has to take a feared course or not graduate. These people are all "between the devil and the deep blue sea."

Client Perception of Conflicts Conflicts and the way individuals perceive them are of utmost importance in their adjustment especially when they have to do with one's perceived capacity to deal with life. The task of the counselor must, then, be concerned with the client's resolution of conflict. (It must be noted, though, that what the counselor sees as a conflict may not be so in the client's eyes.)

Furthermore, the counselor should be aware that a conflict situation may be stimulating a conscious or unconscious recall on the part of the client as to previous unresolved conflicts. The counselor is usually unaware of these. This is not to say that the counselor should emphasize material that is in the client's unconscious or that major emphasis should be placed on childhood experiences. What we are emphasizing is the necessity of the counselor's being aware of past influences on the client's present perception.

Each of us reacts to conflicts in our own individualistic manner depending on a number of factors centering on the core of the self. The central inner conflict is, as Horney (1945) has noted, often a battle between the constructive forces of the real self and the obstructive forces of pride. Put in another fashion. this is a conflict between healthy growth and unhealthy drive.

In order to focus on growth in the counseling relationship it will be necessary, then, for the counselor to make certain inferences regarding the self-concept because of the difference between the *inferred* self-concept of the individual and self-reports obtained from him. In this regard, Combs et al. (1963) have demonstrated that the relationship between the two is minimal. Correlations they obtained between self-report and inferred self-concept ranged from −.119 to +.336 with a mean of .114. The conclusion probably is that we either do not know ourselves well or do not report ourselves accurately to others.

This would lead to the necessity of the counselor getting information about the individual so he/she can make some accurate inferences regarding the client's self-concept through asking such questions as:

"What do you . . .?"
"When do you . . .?"
"What things . . .?"
"What do your friends . . .?"
"Have you had any experiences with . . .?"
"How satisfying was that . . .?"
"Were you successful in . . .?"

These are not the only means of increasing the number of self-reference statements. Other investigators have found that counselor reinforcement of these types of responses (Ince, 1968, pp. 140-146; Kennedy and Zimmer, 1968, pp. 357-362) through such techniques as nods of the head, smiles, and generally affirmative responses will increase these types of statements by the client.

The authentic counselor will keep in mind that the first task is to help create a situation in which the client feels comfortable *talking about him/herself, no matter what the subject—as long as it is personal.* Once this is accomplished the client will unerringly lead the counselor to the area of concern.

Inferring the Self-Concept A useful schema for inferring the self-concept has been devised by Buchheimer and Balogh (1961, p. 110ff). An approach to inferring the self-concept using their classification progresses through several stages of analysis is shown in Figure 4. At the first level, the counselor reviews a tape recording of an

FIGURE 4
Inferring the Self-Concept
(after Buchheimer and Balogh, p. 110, ff.)

Level A. This consists of direct evidence concerning your subject: either quotes or other direct evidence.

I. Perception of Self in General-Effectiveness, status, ideal self	"I have trouble with math and reading. I get bad marks." "I get in trouble a lot, usually for fighting. Sometimes it's not my fault." "I'm two years behind in school." "My father never married my mother." "My mother married my step-father." "My brothers aren't my real brothers, only half-brothers."
II. Perception of Others, environment, social demands, developmental tasks	"My math teacher blames me when it's not my fault. My aunt says I should know better than to act that way." "My step-father fights my mother. She has to run to the hospital sometimes." "My step-father drinks a lot." "My real father asks me questions about them, and they ask about him."
III. Perception of others' reactions to him/her.	"My math teacher is mean. Adults think I'm not trying to do better." "Adults think I'm a lot of trouble." "Kids make fun of me because they find out I'm 12 and in the fourth grade."
IV. Goals and Directions: direction, ambition, purpose	"I should try to do better in school." "I want to get a job to make some money." "I want to make some new friends."
V. Values, Ideals, Beliefs	"He started the fight when he spit at me. I try to stay out of trouble, but sometimes I get mad." "I worry about my mother and about getting in trouble."

Focusing on Growth   41

Level B. What inferences can you make in each of the self-concept areas? What are the dynamics of the situation? Do NOT go beyond your data. This deals with the meanings of the statements in Level A.

I. Self-Perceptions:	A failure in school. Is always in trouble. An illegitimate child. Is different from brothers.
II. Perception of Others:	Adults don't understand. Adults fight. Adults drink. Adults ask a lot of questions.
III. Perception of others' reactions:	Some adults are mean. They think I'm a lot of trouble and that I don't even try to do good. The kids think I'm dumb because I'm two years behind in school.
IV. Goals and Directions:	Wants to do better in school. Wants to get a job. Wants to make new friends.
V. Values and Ideals:	It's wrong to start a fight. It's good to stay out of trouble.

Level C. At this level, integrate and synthesize the inferences you have made at Level B. Make disciplined speculations about your subject that can be substantiated by, or projected from observable behavior #1, infer both the individual's general and vocational self-concept.

_____perceives himself as a failure, and he sees the world as a place of trouble for him. He has few friends and finds that most adults react negatively towards him. His parents do not provide the security he needs as a child. He worries about his mother and about getting in trouble. He wants to stay out of trouble, to do better in school, and to get a job. He has little hope, however, and needs a great deal of support and encouragement.

interview and classifies the client responses into five categories. Then the counselor synthesizes these statements and begins to make inferences about self-concept. Finally, the counselor will make an attempt to synthesize the total amount of information about the client in a unified fashion.

Once the client demonstrates that he/she is ready to begin to take positive steps, the counselor can begin to place emphasis on furthering the growth process in terms of decision making. Often the counselor will find it appropriate to play a catalytic role in the process, asking such questions as, "What do you think it would be like if you...?" and "Suppose you did go into that training course, how do you think you'd do?"

This can readily be seen as an attempt on the part of the counselor to aid the client in realistically appraising strengths and weaknesses in order to determine his/her potential to pursue certain courses of action. In addition, the counselor can aid the client to gain greater self-understanding through focus on the client's goals, values, and attitudes, e.g.:

"Will this plan help you to accomplish what you want?"

"You've mentioned that you want to help people; will this allow you to do that?"

"Do you think you'd be comfortable playing that kind of role?"

The above examples serve to illustrate a means whereby the counselor can help clients evaluate their plans in terms of goals and aid them to appraise their decisions. In addition, it must be emphasized that this type of approach can serve to aid clients in analyzing their own motives and needs. Such discussions can also serve to help clients to grow in terms of their problem-solving and decision making capacity. It is the viewpoint of the authors that true growth on the part of counselees is in terms of becoming mature, independent persons who can solve their own problems and who do not need a counselor. For that reason, the counselor should always keep in mind that he/she is really most concerned about *future* problems or decisions that a client will be facing—not only those with which he/she is presently concerned. This type of attitude will have a great effect on counselor behavior for he/she will then not be apt to be concerned with the quick, facile making of an immediate decision.

Let us reemphasize this point. The true test of a counselor's effectiveness is how well the client functions in the future—when the counselor is not available to help him/her and, indeed, the erstwhile client does not need a counselor at all.

Decision Making in the Interview One major goal of counseling is increased self-responsibility and increased maturity in decision making by the counselee (Van Hoose and Pietrofesa, 1970, p. 12). The counselee is helped to clarify attitudes, values, and desires and to structure them into a "priority hierarchy." The facilitative conditions the counselor offers help establish the necessary growth atmosphere. The counselee is free to explore the meaning of life, what he/she, wants from life and how he/she can deal with possible alternatives in obtaining certain ends. The counselor should remember that the decision making process and any resultant decision is influenced by the counselee's conception of him/herself and the resulting attitudes. The question can be raised at this time as to the appropriate goal of counseling in decision making. Is it the decision making process or the outcome of that process? Dilley (1967) comments as follows:

> The goals of counseling (and for counselors) have to do with helping counselees improve their decision making skills, with facilitating the making of good decisions. Counselors need to know what good decisions are—thus back to our earlier question and a dilemma. The 'goodness' of a decision has been viewed in terms of (1) outcome, how a decision actually turns out, and (2) process, the quality of the deliberations leading to the making of the decision. Neither view is satisfactory in and of itself.[p. 547]

Both process and outcome then become possible goals and a logical focus for the counselor. Peters (1970) states that, "Once thought to be discrete and singular in nature, decision making is now recognized as a part of the developmental process" (p. 79).

The counselor facilitates in certain ways his counselee's decision making. The counselee may be helped to:

> (1) clarify the decision situation, (2) consider the possible alternatives in that situation (3) consider the possible outcomes, (4) estimate the probability and desirability of each outcome for him, and (5) in considering the available information, choose the alternative whose outcomes are

most desirable and presumably most probable. [Dilley, 1968, p. 249]

The proper role of the counselor will be to recognize that the client is often fraught with anxiety regarding the making of a decision. Frequently the best decision may be to *not* make one at all. Above all, it must be emphasized, the counselor should not attempt to hurry the client into a decision and feel a situation has been resolved. Too often, that type of resolution lasts only until the client leaves the counselor's office.

The counselor, therefore, should recognize the fact that a client will often vacillate for several interviews until he/she can determine what course of action to pursue. This may be because of the need for more information or because there is some life situation of which the counselor is unaware. One of the writers is reminded of a client who spent an entire interview resisting an obvious course of action for no apparent reason. It was not until the time period was almost up that she revealed the fact that she was pregnant.

The counselor then accepts the counselee's inability to make a decision and does not criticize or threaten. In displaying his/her own tolerance for ambiguity during the decision making process, the counselor improves the client's ability to deal with feelings of ambiguity. The counselor proceeds "to help the client with the task of identifying the reasons for his inability to decide" (Tyler, 1969, p. 146). The issues may indeed become complex but they probably need identification in order for resolution to occur. Again, the purpose of bringing into focus the reasons for hesitancy is not to inform the counselor but rather to allow the counselee an opportunity to express and deal with them. The counselor at times may also intervene for the client outside of the counseling session. This should be accomplished with permission of the counselee. For example, Ron C. came to the school counselor ostensibly because he was having difficulty in advanced algebra. This troubled Ron, a high school junior, who had stated he wanted to go into engineering school. Ron's school records indicated that since the eighth grade he had not received higher than a "D" in math or science. He also had scored at the fifth percentile or below on his aptitude tests. As counseling proceeded over several weeks, Ron revealed that his father, a retired naval warrant officer (engineer), had insisted upon this occupational goal. Ron didn't want to be an engineer, but felt he would like to enlist in the Navy upon graduation. Ron did not want to talk to his father, who he described as being obstinate and quite volatile in temper. Ron, almost in tears asked the counselor to intercede in his behalf. The counselor acceded and did indeed find the father obstinate and volatile. Tyler (1969) points out that in such interviews with parents the counselor should, "stress the client's positive assets in some field other than the one the parent has chosen rather than attempt directly to argue him out of his insistence on an unwise choice" (p. 147).

Earlier we mentioned the "goodness of a decision." In what light are decisions judged? Tyler (1969) after mentioning "judgments by outsiders" and "how well things work out for the client," finally comes to the criterion of "commitment." She goes on to say:

> A decision is good if the person who makes it is completely willing to take its consequences. In most cases the counselor would hope that the course a client decides to take is one in which he will find success and satisfaction. But...if he is willing to face failure, if and when it confronts him, and is ready to change to a less preferred alternative, if circumstances demand that he do so, who is to say that his decision is a bad one?[p.151]

In aiding the client to progress, the counselor will continually attempt to be open to any "feedback" that might contradict his present perceptions or hypotheses. This, then, will make it necessary for the counselor to be concerned with the *realities* of the situation regardless of his/her own judgments, standards, or values. Only in this fashion will the counselor not expect the client to progress at a faster pace than he/she is either ready or able to proceed. The counselor in order to be able to accomplish this, however, must be able to function as an open, genuine person and cannot achieve such ends in the client without personifying these qualities him/herself.

SUMMARY

Several psychological considerations are presented in order to show that the counselor can focus upon counselee growth in a variety of areas. Self-concept and the individual's knowledge of his/her perceptual field and behavior offer a fertile ground for counselor concentration. Those most in need of help will bring to counseling conflicts of various sorts. The solution of these conflicts helps counselees to reach fulfillment and a state of self-actualization.

It is stressed that the counselor should be concerned with the counselee's future behavior in terms of the counselee's ability to make decisions for him/herself.

REFERENCES

Anderson, C.M.
   1965 "The Self-Image: A Theory of the Dynamics of Behavior." In D. Hamacheck, *The Self in Growth, Teaching and Learning.* Englewood Cliffs, N.J.: Prentice-Hall, pp.1-13.

Boyd, A.J.
   1970 "Self-Concept and its Implication for Counselors." New Orleans: APGA Abstracts, p. 307.

Brooks, R.M.
   1963 "The Self-System: A Sociological Analysis." *Catholic Counselor,* 8:27-30.

Buchheimer, Arnold, and Balogh, Sara.
   1961 *The Counseling Relationship.* Chicago: Science Research Associates.

Cameron, Norman.
   1947 *The Psychology of Behavior.* Boston: Houghton Mifflin.

Carter, T.P.
   1968 "The Negative Self-Concept of Mexican-American Students." *School and Society,* 96:217-219.

Chambers, J., and Lieberman, L.
   1965 "Differences Between Normal and Clinical Groups in Judging, Evaluating and Associating Needs." *Journal of Clinical Psychology,* 21:145-149.

Combs, A.W.
   1962 "A Perceptual View of the Adequate Personality." *Perceiving, Behaving, Becoming.* Yearbook. Washington: Association for Supervision and Curriculum Development.

Combs, A.W., et al.
   1969 *Florida Studies in the Helping Professions.* Gainesville: University of Florida.

Combs, A.W., Courson, C.C. and Soper, D.W.
   1963 "The Measurement of Self-Concept and Self-Report." *Educational and Psychological Measurement,* 23:439-500.

Combs, A.W., and Snygg, D.
   1959 *Individual Behavior.* New York: Harper and Row.

Combs, A.W., and Soper, D.W.
 1963 "The Perceptual Organization of Effective Counselors." *Journal of Counseling Psychology,* 10:222-226.

Combs, C.
 1964 "Perception and Self: Scholastic Underachievement In the Academically Capable."*Personnel and Guidance Journal,* 43:47-51.

Copeland, Elaine
 1977 "Counseling Black Women With Negative Self-Concepts." *Personnel and Guidance Journal,* 55(7), 397-400.

Dilley, J.
 1967 "Decision-Making: A Dilemma and a Purpose for Counseling."*Personnel and Guidance Journal* 45:547-551. Reprinted with permission of the publisher, American Personnel and Guidance Association, Washington D.C.
 1968 "Counselor Actions that Facilitate Decision-Making." *The School Counselor,* 15:247-252. Reprinted with permission of the publisher, American Personnel and Guidance Association, Washington, D.C.

Felker, D.W.
 1974 *Building Positive Self-Concepts.* Minneapolis: Burgess Publishing Co.

Frazier, A., and Combs, A.W.
 1958 "New Horizons in the Field of Research; The Self-Concept." *Educational Leadership,* 15:315-319.

Gale, R.F.
 1969 *Developmental Behavior* New York: Macmillan. By permission of the publisher.

Havighurst, R.J., et al.
 1965 "The Development of the Ideal Self in Childhood and Adolescence." In D. Hamacheck, *The Self in Growth, Teaching and Learning.* Englewood Cliffs, N.J.: Prentice-Hall, pp. 226-239.

Horney, Karen.
 1937 *The Neurotic Personality of Our Times.* New York: Norton.
 1945 *Our Inner Conflicts.* New York: Norton.

Ince, Lawrence.
 1968 "Effects of Fixed-Interval Reinforcement on the Frequency of a Verbal Response Class in a Quasi-Counseling Situation." *Journal of Counseling Psychology,* 15:140-146.

Jersild, A.T.
 1965 "Social and Individual Origins of Self." In D. Hamacheck, *The Self in Growth, Teaching, and Learning.* Englewood Cliffs, N.J.: Prentice-Hall, pp. 209-225.

Kennedy, John, and Zimmer, Jules.
 1968 "Reinforcing Value of Five Stimulus Conditions in a Quasi-Counseling Situation." *Journal of Counseling Psychology,* 15:357-362.

Korman, A.K.
 1967 "Self Esteem as a Moderator of the Relationship Between Self-Per-

ceived Abilities and Vocational Choice." *Journal of Applied Psychology,* 51:65-67.

Lecky, P.
1961 *Self-Consistency: A Theory of Personality.* Hamden, Conn.: The Shoe String Press, Inc.

Leonard, G., Pietrofesa J.J., and Bank, I.
1969 "A Workshop for the Improvement of the Self-Concepts of Inner-City Youngsters." *The School Counselor,* 16:375-379. Reprinted with permission of the publisher, American Personnel and Guidance Association, Washington, D.C.

Lowther, M.A.
1963 "Academic Achievement and Self-Esteem. *University of Michigan School of Education Bulletin.* 35:7-11.

McDaniels, C.
1968 "Youth: Too Young to Choose?"*Vocational Guidance Quarterly,* 16:242-249.

Maslow, A.H.
1954 Motivation and Personality. New York: Harper and Row.

1962 "Some Basic Propositions of a Growth and Self-Actualization Psychology." In Arthur W. Combs ,ed. *Perceiving, Behaving, Becoming.* Yearbook. Washington: Association for Supervision and Curriculum Development.

May, R.
1967 *Psychology and the Human Dilemma,* Princeton: D.Van Nostrand. Copyright © 1967 by Litton Educational Publishing Inc. By permission of D. Van Nostrand.

Merrill, F.E.
1965 "Social Selves and Social Problems." *Journal of Sociology and Social Research,* 49:389-400

Patterson, C.H.
1957 "Theories of Vocational Choice and the Emotionally Disturbed Client." *Educational and Psychological Measurement,* 17:377-390.

1970 "A Model for Counseling and Other Facilitative Human Relationships." In W. Van Hoose, and J. Pietrofesa, eds. *Counseling and Guidance in the Twentieth Century.* Boston: Houghton Mifflin, pp. 251-265.

Peters, H.J.
1970 *The Guidance Process.* Itasca, Ill.: F.E. Peacock.

Pietrofesa, J.J.
1969 "Self-Concept: A Vital Factor in School and Career Development." *Clearing House,* 44:37-40.

Rogers, C.R.
- 1958 *On Becoming a Person.* Austin: The Hogg Foundation for Mental Hygiene, University of Texas.
- 1968 "The Significance of the Self-Regarding Attitudes and Perceptions." In C. Gordon, and K. Gergen, *The Self in Social Interaction,* New York: Wiley, pp. 435-442.

Rosenthal, Robert, and Jacobson, Lenore.
- 1968 *Pygmalion in the Classroom.* New York: Holt, Rinehart, and Winston.

Snyder, R.T.
- 1966 "Personality Adjustment, Self-Attitudes and Anxiety Differences in Retarded Adolescents." *American Journal of Mental Deficiency,* 71:33-41.

Thorne, Frederick C.
- 1967 "The Etiological Equation." In R.R. Carkhuff, and B.G. Berenson, *Beyond Counseling and Therapy.* New York: Holt, Rinehart and Winston, pp. 235-272.

Truax, Charles, and Carkhuff, Robert.
- 1967 *Toward Effective Counseling and Psychotherapy.* Chicago: Aldine.

Tyler, L.
- 1969 *The Work of the Counselor.* New York: Appleton-Century-Crofts, Educational Division, Meredith Corporation.

Van Hoose, W.H., and Pietrofesa, J.J.
- 1970 *Counseling and Guidance in the Twentieth Century.* Boston: Houghton Mifflin.

Chapter 3 The Counseling Relationship

In some systems of counseling the process of helping is viewed as almost synonymous with the relationship that exists between counselor and counselee. Thus, Rogers (1961) states:

> If I can provide a certain type of relationship, the other person will discover within himself the capacity to use that relationship for growth, and change and personal development will occur.[p. 33]

Rogers' "certain relationship" includes genuineness, liking and accepting the client, and a sensitive empathy with the client's feelings. The development of an effective counseling relationship involves being natural, opening communication, reducing anxiety, communicating a feeling of acceptance, developing rapport, and establishing a tentative goal for counseling. These counselor behaviors help the counselee to clarify what counseling is about and how it can help him/her deal with specific concerns.

The attributes of an ideal counseling relationship are friendliness, warmth, and a comfortable closeness between counselor and client. Other characteristics are implied, e.g., permissiveness, acceptance, and safety.

Shertzer and Stone (1968, p. 8) emphasize counselor-client interaction as an aspect of the helping relationship. They note:

> Each participant is affected by the other's verbal and nonverbal communication. The helper and the person helped observe and involve each other's interest and attention. Each talks, reacts, responds to the other verbally and nonverbally, and both kinds of behavior have current and residual impact. Nonverbal behavior—facial expressions, gestures, body motions—may relate directly to verbal content or to affective experiences.

Descriptions of the helping relationship are sufficiently broad to include a wide variety of services in several occupations. However, the term has a special meaning for counselors and there is some common agreement on the centrality of the relationship in effective counseling. Truax and Carkhuff (1967, p. 31) write:

> The theories of practitioners who represent a variety of therapeutic and counseling approaches converge upon the central therapeutic ingredients of a helping 'relationship.' To be sure, their emphases vary, and there are large and small differences in the exact meaning of the constructs involved. Further, they diverge in many ways on other issues. It is perhaps worthwhile to repeat that the central ingredients of empathy, warmth, and genuineness do not merely represent techniques of psychotherapy or counseling, but are interpersonal skills that the counselor or therapist employs in applying his 'technique' or 'expert knowledge,' whether he is a psychotherapist, a vocational rehabilitation counselor, or a personnel counselor.

There is yet another factor which needs consideration in our treatment of the counseling relationship. In practice, helping another person requires that the counselor give attention to facilitating the client's personal development. To be facilitative requires that the counselor be sensitive to the other person's feelings, and try to understand him/her. Respect, acceptance, warmth, and concern for the client are basic to the facilitative process. Further, when the counselor is truly facilitative the client is able to utilize his/her full potential necessary to achieve maximum growth.

SOME CHARACTERISTICS OF A COUNSELING RELATIONSHIP
Until recently most of the literature on the counseling relationship was based upon the clinical experience of counselors or therapists. With a few exceptions these conditions hold true at the present time. However, three very significant studies are relevant to our present discussion and the conclusions from these studies are summarized below.

Fiedler's (1950) research in counseling proceeded from the assumption that the relationship is the most important element in counseling. He found that experienced counselors with different theoretical positions tended to be in close agreement on the ideal counseling relationship. Further, Fiedler discovered that lay people could describe a good therapeutic relationship almost as well as the therapists. He concluded that a good counseling relationship may be but a variation of any good interpersonal relationship. Martin et al. (1966), studying professional counselors, found that while professional counselors as a group demonstrated significantly higher condition levels than friends, the counselors also differed from each other, suggesting that while professional experience may be of primary import in the development of receptor and communication skills, other factors such as the personality and beliefs of the counselor may be critical (pp. 441-446).

A third significant study, the research of Combs (1969) and his associates, also provides significant information on the complex problems of a client-counselor relationship. Their studies on the characteristics of a desirable helper was based on the premise that the effective helping relationship will be a function of the effective use of the helper's self in bringing about the fulfillment of his/her own and society's purposes.

Twenty-nine counselor trainees in a National Defense Education Act (NDEA) Institute were enrolled in a course in Personality Dynamics. Each student was required to turn in four personal "Human Relations Incidents" during the semester including a critique covering (1) what he/she thought about it at the time, (2) what seemed to be the crux of the problem, and (3) what he/she now felt should have been done about it.

Judges then evaluated the anonymous reports in terms of the following perceptual variables, of which the first of each pair is considered the desirable characteristic of the "helper."

A. With respect to their general perceptual orientations, good counselors will be more likely to perceive:
 1. From an internal rather than from an external frame of reference.
 2. In terms of people rather than things.

B. With respect to their perceptions of other people, good counselors will perceive others as:
 1. Able rather than unable.
 2. Dependable rather than undependable.
 3. Friendly rather than unfriendly.
 4. Worthy rather than unworthy.

C. With respect to their perceptions of other people, good counselors will perceive themselves as:
 1. Identifying with people rather than being apart from them.
 2. Having enough rather than wanting.
 3. Self-revealing rather than self-concealing.

D. With respect to purposes, good counselors will perceive their purposes as:
 1. Freeing rather than controlling.
 2. Altruistic rather than narcissistic.
 3. Concerned with larger rather than smaller meanings.
 [Combs et al., 1969, pp. 21-27]

Jackson and Thompson (1971) found that most effective counselors were more positive in their attitudes toward self, clients, and counseling. They felt that "whether or not counselors view and act toward . . . most clients as being friendly or unfriendly, able or unable, worthy or unworthy is related to a counselor's effectiveness" (p 252).

Rogers' (1958) description of the helping relationship provides further information of the kinds of counselor characteristics that accelerate growth in the client. After reviewing a number of studies on helping relationships, Rogers concluded: "It seems clear that relationships which are helpful have different characteristics from relationships which are unhelpful" (p. 11). Rogers suggests a number of questions which counselors may ask themselves as they approach a counseling relationship. His ten questions are:

1. Can I be in some way, which will be perceived by the other person, trustworthy, dependable, or consistent in some deep sense?
2. Can I be expressive enough as a person that what I am will be communicated unambiguously?
3. Can I let myself experience positive attitudes toward this other person—attitudes of warmth, caring, liking, interest, respect?
4. Can I be strong enough as a person to be separate from the other?
5. Am I secure enough as a person to permit the other person his/her separateness?
6. Can I let myself enter fully into the world of this person's feelings and personal meanings and see these as he/she does?
7. Can I receive the other person as he/she is? Can I communicate this attitude?
8. Can I act with sufficient sensitivity in the relationship that my behavior will not be perceived as a threat?
9. Can I free the other person from the threat of external evaluation?
10. Can I meet this other individual as a person who is in the process of *becoming*, or will I be bound by his/her past and by my past?

Inherent in the helping relationship is the mutual compatibility of roles of the client and the counselor. Such conditions as mutuality, trust, and empathy must permeate all good counseling relationships.

The client is expected to commit some time, energy and attention to be a recipient of counseling. Further, if he/she enters into the relationship, he/she must also trust the counselor as a person who can help. Likewise, the counselor commits his/her time and energies toward helping the client change his/her behavior. Together helper and client must create a system in interaction based upon mutual dependence, each contributing a share so that the counselor is able to intervene and the client is able to profit from the intervention (Maier, 1965, p. 211).

ESTABLISHING THE RELATIONSHIP

Rapport Rapport is one of the internal conditions which most experts see as essential to the development of a good counseling climate. It is an intangible, characterized by sincerity, pleasantness, and interest—all factors that are difficult to measure.

When there is good rapport the client talks freely about him/herself and his/her real problems. Because the development of a good working relationship must begin with the initial contact, many of the suggestions in the literature on establishing rapport deal with the first interview. However, the counselor must be concerned with maintaining rapport throughout the relationship.

Counseling rapport is a dynamic, changing entity and as such varies from session to session even with the same counselee. The counselor helps to establish rapport by accepting the counselee. This point needs to be clarified for almost immediately someone will raise the question, "If you accept the counselee, you are in essence giving approval of some of the unacceptable behaviors in which he/she is engaged." The counselor accepts the counselee as a worthwhile individual—a person with respect and dignity who has the right to make choices for him/herself. This, then, is not to say that acceptance implies approval of specific behaviors. In fact, the authentic counselor (see chapter 4) may very well in effect say, "I do not necessarily approve of your behavior, but I grant you the right to make decisions for yourself—decisions for which you must accept the responsibility." Acceptance provides an atmosphere where problems can be worked through without anxieties created by rejection of self as a human being.

The counselee comes to feel secure not as a result of counselor approval, but from something much more basic, i.e., a thoroughly consistent acceptance. In the safety of such an encounter, he/she moves from the cognitive dimensions of interaction into the affective domain.

He/She perhaps comes to express attitudes he/she has been unable to cope with because of feeling that they were unacceptable or even repugnant to others. Defenses may be withdrawn and certain aspects of behavior are clarified for the first time. The counselor has essentially helped to move the counselee from perceiving and experiencing him/herself as unworthy, unacceptable, and unlovable to the realization that he/she is respected and can behave in a healthy manner. More effective behaviors result.

We are somewhat wary of formulas or a "bag-of-tricks" method for establishing rapport or for getting started. In our view, it is hazardous and perhaps naive for the counselor to open a conversation with such statements as, "How I can help you?" or "Tell me your problem." The client may not be certain of the answer to either of these questions. Counselors too often feel that they must talk—even at the risk of creating resistance in the client.

We do not mean to give the impression that it is always easy for the counselor to accept the counselee and develop the necessary rapport. The counselor must work at it in many respects. In some cases the counselor may have to refer the client to someone else. One case comes to mind almost immediately in which one of the authors was a practicum advisor. A white, female counselor-trainee, Mrs. Smith, attempted to establish a counseling relationship with a fifteen-year-old black male. She was met with complete hostility and absolute silence. The counselee did not even look at the counselor for two sessions. As a consequence, the counselor became increasingly hostile. Finally, initiating a third session, she mentioned that things had not progressed well and that perhaps it was best that another counselor be made available. The counselee did not respond. As Mrs. Smith left the room to get the counselor, the young man leaned over and spoke his first words, "You can go to hell." She returned, introduced the counselee to Mr. Jones, a black twenty-five-year-old, and departed. Mr. Jones was a counselor able to accept the hostility of this young man. The change in counselee behavior over just a short period of time was quite dramatic. Rogers (1951) states:

> The therapist . . . must concentrate on purpose only — that of providing deep understanding and acceptance of the attitudes consciously held at this moment by the client as he

explores step by step into the dangerous areas which he has been denying . . . [p. 30].

This acceptance, most importantly, must be genuine and sensitive. The counselor cannot express it; the counselee experiences it. Early in his training one of the authors had an experience which cured his habit of verbally dominating the interview. After a conference with the mother of a young client, the supervisor asked the counselor-intern to stop by his office. The following dialogue ensued:

Supervisor: I saw your interview with Mrs. ——.
Intern: Yes! [Expecting a compliment]
Supervisor: [Handing intern a box] I bought you a box of jawbreakers. The next time you feel you must talk so much, try these.
Intern: Uh, but . . .
Supervisor: See you tomorrow.

In most cases when an adolescent or an adult comes for counseling, it is safe to assume that the client has some knowledge of why he/she is there and can therefore be expected to verbalize his/her concerns without undue prompting from the counselor. It is recognized that in schools clients are often referred by teachers and administrators and they may not always be eager for the services of counseling. In fact, they may be resistant or hostile. In such instances the counselor may need to explain his/her role and offer to help if such help is desired. The client has the option of accepting or rejecting counseling.

There are, of course, times in counseling, even in self-referred clients, when small talk may be necessary to get started. Such statements as the following may serve this purpose: "I would like to get to know you better; why don't you tell me a little about yourself." "Gee, it's a nice day. Have you been outside?" or "I have seen you around, and I'm glad to get a chance to talk with you."

Special Considerations With Children With young children the technique of getting started and continuing an effective counseling relationship may require considerable variation from traditional approaches. To be explicit, understandings from counseling with adolescents or adults, or from work with disturbed children in nonschool settings may not be applicable to counseling children in the school. The first requirement is that counselors who work with children should know something of the characteristics and nature of children.

The same conditions that make for effective counseling relationships with adult and adolescent clients are equally valid when counseling with children. In spite of the young client's close relationship with parents and teachers, the counselor's trust in the client's potential for coping with his/her environment and his/her interpersonal relationships remains firm The fact is that many children benefit from counseling without concur rent consultation with significant adults. It is obvious that some children cannot cope with their problems alone. In such cases work with parents and teachers is a necessity.

The counselor who works with children may need to assume greater responsibility for developing a counseling relationship than would be required in a relationship with older clients. Often children do verbalize their feelings and concerns during counseling and they assume some responsibility for the counseling interview (Van Hoose, 1966). However, Mann (1967) found that in actual interviews with children, elementary school counselors tend to help children identify specific topics discussed during counseling. She believes that in counseling, children tend to discuss concerns in a global sort of way, and that the counselor finds it necessary to help them pinpoint their real concern.

Hawkins (1967) investigated the topics that children discuss with counselors. She found that the three topics most frequently discussed were related to home, school, and self. She reports that children in both the upper and lower elementary grades were able to verbalize their concerns during counseling.

Getting the counseling process underway with young children requires the ability to communicate in the language of the child and the flexibility to use a variety of approaches and responses. In our experience, some children come to counseling quite ready and eager to talk, while others sit or stand in silence. The following brief excerpts illustrate the two extremes. The first case is a seven-year-old second grader.

> *Client:* Miss G——[*As he walked in*] look what I done today.
> *Counselor:* Oh, a picture. And you did that?
> *Client:* Yes. Miss H—— let us paint, and I made three things ... I made uh, I made a space rocket, and a mummy like I saw in the museum, and a

clown. And you know our bulletin board; you know, where things are up; Miss H——she said I could put one up there. And guess what else, I got to carry the flag today.

Counselor: Gee, you have been doing a lot of things lately.

Client: Yeah, and I used all colors, too, and Miss H —— said, she said next week we could make cards, for mothers you know.

The silent case, Mark, is nine years old and in grade four.

Counselor: Hi, Mark, How are you?
Client: O.K.
Counselor: O.K. Uh, what's been happening lately?
Client: [*short pause*] Nothin'.
Counselor: Any good things?
Client: Uh, uh.
Counselor: Bad things?
Client: Uh, uh.
Counselor: Gee, Mark, you don't seem very happy? Something wrong?
Client: Uh, uh.
Counselor: [*After brief pause*] I like your shirt today. Is that new?
Client: Yeah. My sister sent it.
Counselor: That made you happy, I bet.
Client: Uh, huh.
Counselor: Some things make you happy—like a new shirt from your sister, right?
Client: Yeah, I guess.
Counselor: But you don't seem happy now? Want to tell me about it?
Client: They threw my hat in the water and we had a big fight.

The problem in interviews with silent or reluctant clients is that they turn into a monologue or a question-and-answer session. Open and honest statements by the counselor can help such interviews develop into two-person discussions.

Trust Mutual trust and respect are critical elements in the counseling relationship. Without these elements, very little that is really positive will be accomplished.

Saying to the client "You can trust me," "I respect you," etc., may not help unless the counselee actually senses that this is true. If such conditions are clearly present, it is not necessary to put them in words.

These conditions are created in some measure by counselor attention to what the counselee is saying, by counselor attitudes, by dealing with client feelings, and by demonstrating that the counselor is making a genuine attempt to understand the client. Facial expressions, body gestures, and the tone of the counselor's voice also contribute. Professional competence is, of course, a factor in creating a condition of trust and respect. Beyond this, the self of the counselor becomes a most important element.

Empathy in the Counseling Relationship Empathy in a counseling relationship involves at least two components. One is a cognitive component that involves psychological understanding. The other is an affective component of feeling with a person (Blocher, 1966, p. 146).

The concept of empathy involves the counselor's ability to perceive and communicate, accurately and with sensitivity, the feelings of the client and the meanings of those feelings. By communicating, "I understand" and "I am beginning to see and feel with you," the counselor facilitates the client's movement toward a deeper self-awareness and a knowledge of the client's feelings and experiences (Truax and Carkhuff, 1967, p. 285).

Over the years, Rogers (1951; 1975) has provided several definitions and lucid descriptions of the meaning of empathy. Empathy means entering the world of the client and feeling at home in it. It involves being sensitive to the feelings of the counselee, being alert, moment to moment, to anxiety, fear, or tenderness. It means temporarily living in his/her life, moving in it delicately, without making judgments about it. Empathy means sensing meanings but not trying to uncover feelings of which the counselee is totally unaware, since this may be too threatening. Accurate empathy requires frequent checking with the client to test the accuracy of the counselor's perceptions of what he/she is feeling, and it means that the counselor is guided by these responses (Rogers, 1975, p. 4).

To elaborate upon these points, the concept of empathy also means sensitivity to the world of the client and the personal meanings that his/her own experiences have for him/her. What many clients are looking for is someone to understand. And yet empathy involves much more than a simple understanding of the client. It involves warmth, spontaneity, and the capacity to be with the client both at the cognitive and at the affective level. Patterson (1969) states:

> Empathy involves at least three aspects or stages. Assuming that the client is willing to allow the counselor to enter his private world, it is first necessary that the counselor listen to the client, and make it possible for the client to communicate his perceptions. It involves a sensitive listening from an internal frame of reference rather than from an external frame of reference ... The second aspect of empathy is the counselor's understanding of this world and third is the communication of this understanding to the client. [p. 16]

Means (1973) notes that there are a number of elements in additive empathy:

1. Client's Accurately Expressed Feeling or Obvious Feeling—While this by itself may not be therapeutic, it does facilitate the building of a relationship.

2. Identification of Environmental Stimulus—The stimulus for the feeling needs to be defined.

3. Identification of Client's Behavior Pattern—Behavior patterns are identified in concise, descriptive terms.

4. Feelings toward Self as a Result of Interaction with the Environment—Feelings toward the self are more important than feelings toward others in counseling. If they can be identified they are more likely to lead to behavior change in the client

5. Expectations of Self—Satisfy such expectations, determine how the client feels about self.

6. Basic Beliefs about Self—Beliefs about self lead to either adaptive or maladaptive behavior.

There is some empirical evidence that demonstrates the importance of empathy to counseling outcomes. Dickenson and Truax (1966) reported a positive relationship between empathy, as measured by the Accurate Empathy Scale, and the desired counseling outcome of improvement of academic achievement. The results were obtained in a college counseling center with one counselor working with forty-eight underachieving college freshmen. Lesser (1961), utilizing two measures of empathy, found a positive relationship between the Empathic Understanding Scale and self-concept improvement. Hountras and Anderson (1969) had nine doctoral candidates counseling with fifty-four college students at the University of North Dakota Counseling Center. They once again found a positive relationship between the Accurate Empathy Scale and client self-exploration. Altmann (1973) reported that more increased levels of accurate empathy were provided in cases of clients who continued in counseling than for clients who left.

On the other hand, Katz (1962), Gonyea (1963), and Kratchovil, Aspy, and Carkhuff (1967) found little relationship between empathy and counseling outcomes. Several important considerations arise for counselors. First, it should be understood that differences probably arise as a result of different methodological procedures, measurement instruments, and counseling outcomes. Second, and perhaps most crucial, is that empathy alone might not be sufficient in itself to provide positive counseling outcomes. Gladstein (1970) emphasizes the point that more research needs to be done regarding empathy in counseling, rather than in psychotherapy. He says:

> Additional research concerning counseling and empathy should be carried out. We are in great need of studies of counseling product-outcomes ... These studies should be with normal subjects who bring developmental types of needs to counselors, not hospital or clinic patients. A variety of outcomes—educational, vocational, and personal-social—should be measured. [p. 827]

Communication There is some research evidence which points to a positive relationship between effective communication and good therapeutic conditions. Additionally, it has been suggested that warmth and personal involvement of the communicator has positive influence upon the recipient (Truax and Carkhuff, 1967, p. 119).

It may sound absurd, but without communication there is no counseling. Rogers (1961) states that counseling is good communication, with and between individuals. He adds, "We may also turn the statement around and it will still be true. Good communication, free communication, within, or between men, is always therapeutic" (p. 330).

In another vein, Rogers notes, "The task of psychotherapy is to help the person achieve, through a special relationship with a therapist, good communication within himself. Once this is achieved, he can communicate more freely and more effectively with others" (1961, p. 330).

There are numerous factors that can hinder or foster communication in counseling. Benjamin (1969, pp. 90-91) believes that our own need to judge, to evaluate, to confirm or deny constitutes a major barrier to good communication. He believes that if counselors minimize the client's concern, tell him/her that he/she is probably wrong, or if the counselor states he/she dislikes something liked by the client, communication will be impaired.

In a similar vein, Gordon (1972) describes twelve categories of statements which stifle communication. Gordon's list ("the dirty dozen") includes: (1) ordering, directing, commanding; (2) warning, admonishing, threatening; (3) moralizing, preaching, obliging; (4) advising, giving suggestions; (5) persuading, arguing, lecturing; (6) judging, blaming, criticizing; (7) evaluating, approving; (8) name-calling, ridiculing, shaming; (9) interpreting, analyzing, diagnosing; (10) reassuring, consoling; (11) probing, questioning, interrogating; and (12) withdrawing, humoring, and distracting.

Gordon describes several alternative methods of communication. One of these is *active listening*, which conveys back to the counselee that you hear and understand him/her. Active listening promotes a relationship of warmth between counselor and counselee, and helps counselees deal with their feelings (Gordon, 1972, pp. 10-13).

Other counselor behaviors that impair communication include "verbal hemorrhages" (the counselor's), note-taking during the interview, restlessness, and inattentiveness. Clients have a right to talk during counseling, and the professional counselor will listen. The client also has a valid claim on the complete attention of the counselor. To illustrate this point, we quote a seventeen-year-old youth who was a member of a student panel discussing counseling in the school.

He's always busy. I go to see him and maybe get in for five minutes. Once I was there and that cat called somebody on the phone and talked with them most of the time. Counselors don't have much time to see students.

Listening and hearing clearly what is said is one key to good communication. Some counselors become so concerned over their own role in the interview that they cannot listen effectively. Trying to decide what to do next while the client is talking is a clear obstacle to communication.

Does this mean, then, that the counselor should not be concerned about what to say or do in the interview? Obviously not, but thinking of what to say should not take place while the counselee is talking. When the counselor really listens, almost inevitably a moment's silence will intervene between the client's pause and the counselor's response. Whatever the counselor says or does will be unpremeditated. It may not be polished, but it will be genuine (Benjamin, 1969, p. 103).

How can effective communication be fostered? In a sense, this chapter has already described several counselor behaviors that foster communication. However, some specific factors that make for good communication need to be emphasized.

It ought to be clear that the counselor must understand his/her clients. By understanding, we mean depth knowledge of the characteristics and behaviors of that age group, something of their life experiences, their cultural background, their life space. The counselor must also be acquainted with the persisting needs and concerns of his/her clients and their general perceptions of their life experiences.

A genuine and personal concern and a deep interest in the client as a whole person in his/her own right is also a prerequisite for effective communication as it is for good counseling. The ability to listen and to respond to the *feeling* as well as the *content* of what the client says during the interview is also a critical element in communication. The expression of feeling in the interview and the ability of the counselor to deal with the client's feelings, whether they are negative or positive, constitutes one of the most important dimensions in counseling.

An additional important element in communication involves what Robinson (1050, p. 74) describes as dealing with the core of the client's remark. In this connection, the counselor should respond to the point that most interests the client or to the last remark of the feeling contained in the client's statement. The counselor must avoid a response that has little relationship to the client's topic and only in rare instances should the counselor introduce a new topic.

Structuring the Relationship The counseling relationship has its beginning at the moment of the actual meeting of counselor and counselee. From this point on the person seeking help begins to size up his/her part in the relationship and the counselor begins to appraise client status and make some determination of his/her own potential involvement. Client and counselor reach a mutual understanding of their joint state of dependence. As Shertzer and Stone (1968) put it:

> Although varying amounts of freedom are given to the person to be helped, he must have an opportunity to respond and be expansive. Structure varies, depending upon the type of helping relationship but its essential features—patterns of stimuli and response—are always present. Structure enables the relationship to eventuate in growth and productivity. In reality, responsibility for the structure is reciprocal. Both the helper and the person to be helped have needs—to achieve, to be recognized, to be adequate—that determine structure and set in motion responses which the helping person must be prepared to meet if he is to build a helping relationship. [p. 9]

Most clients have some preconceived notions about what happens in counseling. The client may assume that the counselor will give advice, solve problems, or answer questions. It is a sad, but true, statement that too often the client entering a school counselor's office may expect to get a verbal "working over." In any case, it is the responsibility of the counselor to initiate a discussion of what counseling consists of. Thus, *structuring* consists of a joint understanding and agreement upon the boundaries of counseling. It may involve time and physical limitations. For example, the counselor may explain to the very aggressive small child that he/she is free to hit the punching bag, but he/she is not permitted to hit the counselor. For to do otherwise, the counselor may find it difficult to "love" that youngster. Structuring, however, is not a process that takes place only during the initial interview. As counseling progresses, the counselor may see a need to repeat or to restructure the relationship. During the structuring process, the client is also free to express his/her own feelings and attitudes regarding the relationship.

The Real Relationship   The counselor should be two things to his/her clients. First, he/she should be a *real* person to them, and second, he/she should help them repair or resolve problems that have occurred as a result of some developmental failure (Kell and Burow, 1970, p. 116). Personal growth is facilitated when the counselor is "real"; when clients are permitted to know him/her as human, and when he/she is openly genuine in relationships with clients.

Rogers (1967, p. 229) uses the term "congruence" to describe this condition. To Rogers, counselor congruence means without artificiality, without front or facade. In a similar vein, Truax and Carkhuff (1967, p. 32) emphasize that counselors must be spontaneously themselves, deeply genuine, and authentic with their clients.

There is no alternative to congruence in counseling. The client can easily see beyond the "front" of the counselor and the artificiality or phoniness that arises from such a condition will seriously impair counseling effectiveness. (See chapter 6 for a more extensive treatment of authenticity in the counseling relationship.)

Counselor Attitudes   Reference has already been made to the influence of counselor behaviors upon the counseling relationship and consequently upon counseling outcomes. It needs to be emphasized, however, that the actual behavior of the counselor in the interview will reflect his/her attitudes toward the client. Rogers (1958) has used such terms as warmth, caring, liking, interest, and respect to pinpoint some attitudes of the counselor. Whether the counselor is able to create a climate sufficiently free for the client to explore a variety of feelings depends on how well the counselor can demonstrate positive attitudes toward the client.

Rogers (1951) believes that the counselor should be concerned more with attitudes than with specific techniques of counseling. His remarks on the ideal counseling relationship are paraphrased as follows:

Most Characteristic
   The counselor is able to participate completely in the client's communication.

Very Characteristic

The counselor's comments are always right in line with what the client is trying to convey.

The counselor sees the client as a co worker on a common problem.

The counselor sees the counselee as an equal.

The counselor is able to understand the client's feelings.

The counselor tries to understand the client's feelings

The counselor always follows the counselee's line of thought.

The counselor's tone of voice conveys the complete ability to share the counselee's feelings. [pp. 53-54]

The case of Laura may help to illustrate the above points. Laura, a college freshman, was referred to the counseling center by the head resident. She did not make the first appointment. The following day she called the receptionist, explained that she had broken the appointment because she did not feel well. She was given a second appointment which she also failed to keep. A few days later she phoned the receptionist, apologized for breaking the appointment, and stated that she had talked with the resident counselor who assured her there was nothing to be afraid of. She was given a third appointment which she kept.

When she met with her counselor for the first time she quickly communicated her anxiety. The following excerpt is from a tape recording of that first interview.

Counselor: I'm glad we could get together. [*Pause*] I hope we can talk freely in here.

Client: Uh huh. [*Pause*] I don't know what to say ... I'm kinda nervous. I ... I ...

Counselor: I think I know what you're thinking. You are not sure about being here. [*Pause*] You are just a little uneasy about the whole thing.

Client: Well, I don't know what they told you. Uh, I know I have some problems, but ... well, I don't know you. I came because Miss ⎯⎯ thought it would help.

Counselor: I understand. Well, they didn't tell me very much. Uh, sometimes, ah, I don't know you very well, either: but I would like to. I would like to help you in any way I can.

Client: Uh, huh. [*Short pause*] It's so unreal, really. I used to, in high school, kids would come to me to talk about their problems. Now it's me, and I don't know whether I can talk about them or not.

Counselor: Sometimes it is hard to talk about things, but as I said, I hope we can talk and that you will feel free to, to, uh, tell me some things that maybe I can help you with. [*Pause*]

Client: Well, I don't think it's all that bad, but Miss —— thinks I ought to see somebody. She's about the only person over there I can talk to. Hardly any of the girls talk to me or even like me. [*Nervously*] Not many people like me I guess.

Counselor: I've just met you, but I like you, and I'm willing to talk with you.

Whatever the counselor felt in the early remarks of the client, and in spite of the redundancy of some of his remarks, he did sincerely attempt to communicate a positive attitude toward her. The behavior and dynamics of the counselor entered this relationship quite early and perhaps as a result of some anxieties of the client. It is extremely important during the initial interview that the counselor demonstrate his/her willingness to enter into a helping relationship. In the above case, when the counselor indicated that he liked Laura and verbalized his willingness to help her, she began to describe more freely some of her concerns and feelings about others and later about herself.

SUMMARY

We have reached the point in our discussion where it may be helpful to summarize some of the elements and criteria in an effective counseling relationship. We need also to keep in mind the effects of counselor behavior upon counseling outcomes.

The characteristics of a good counseling relationship include genuineness, liking the client, and a sensitive empathy with client feelings. Good counselors perceive their clients as being able, dependable, and worthy. They see themselves as facilitating persons, concerned more with others than with themselves. The good counselor is able to give of him/herself and to participate fully in the counseling relationship.

Effective counseling requires a climate sufficiently free for the client to explore his/her feelings and deal with a variety of concerns. The behavior of the counselor is a major factor in the development of such a climate. Put another way, effective counseling requires a counselor who is open, caring, and interested, and who has the security and the ability to share client feelings. Counselor attitudes are more important than counseling techniques.

REFERENCES

Altmann, H.A.
    1973 "Effects of Empathy, Warmth, and Genuineness in the Initial Counseling Interview." *Counselor Education and Supervision*, 12(3), 225-228.

Benjamin, Alfred.
    1969 *The Helping Interview*. Boston: Houghton Mifflin.

Blocher, Donald H.
    1966 *Developmental Counseling*. New York: The Ronald Press.

Combs, A. W., et al.
    1969 *Florida Studies in the Helping Professions*. Monograph No. 37. Gainesville: University of Florida.

Dickenson, W. A., and Truax, C. B.
    1966 "Group Counseling With College Underachievers." *Personnel and Guidance Journal*, 45:243-247.

Fiedler, Fred.
    1950 "The Concept of an Ideal Therapeutic Relationship." *Journal of Consulting Psychology*, 14:239-245.

Gladstein, Gerald A.
    1970 "Is Empathy Important in Counseling?" *Personnel and Guidance Journal*, 48:827-832.

Gonyea, G. G.
    1963 "The 'Ideal Therapeutic Relationship' and Counseling Outcome." *Journal of Clinical Psychology*, 19:481-487.

Gordon, Thomas.
    1972 "Teacher Effectiveness Training." Solona Beach, Cal.: Effectiveness Training Associates.

Hawkins, Sue.
    1967 "The Content of Elementary Counseling Interviews." *Elementary School Guidance and Counseling*, 2:114-120.

Hountras, P. T., and Anderson, D. L.
    1969 "Counselor Conditions for Self-Exploration of College Students." *Personnel and Guidance Journal*, 48:45-48.

Jackson, M. and Thompson, C.L.
   1971 "Effective Counselor: Characteristics and Attitudes." *Journal of Counseling Psychology,* 18(3), 249-254.

Katz, B.
   1962 *Predictive and Behavioral Empathy and Client Change in Short-term Counseling.* New York: New York University. Unpublished doctoral dissertation.

Kell, Bill L., and Burow, Josephine M.
   1970 *Developmental Counseling and Therapy.* Boston: Houghton Mifflin.

Kratchovil, D., Aspy, D., and Carkhuff, R. A.
   1967 "The Differential Effects of Absolute Level and the Direction of Counselor Change in Level of Functioning over Counseling upon Client Level of Functioning." *Journal of Clinical Psychology,* 23:216-218.

Lesser, W. M.
   1961 "The Relationship Between Counseling Progress and Empathic Understanding." *Journal of Counseling Psychology,* 8:330-336.

Maier, Henry W.
   1965 *Three Theories of Child Development.* New York: Harper and Row.

Mann, Irene.
   1967 "In-Counseling Behavior of Children." Mimeographed. Detroit: Wayne State University.

Martin, J. C., Carkhuff, R. R., and Berenson, Bernard G.
   1966 "Process Variables in Counseling and Psychotherapy." *Journal of Counseling Psychology,* 13:441-446.

Means, B. L.
   1973 "Levels of Empathic Response." *Personnel and Guidance Journal.* 52(1), 23-28.

Patterson, Cecil H.
   1969 "A Current View of Client-Centered or Relationship Therapy." *The Counseling Psychologist,* 1:2-24.

Robinson, Francis P.
   1950 *Principles and Procedures in Student Counseling.* New York: Harper and Brothers.

Rogers, Carl R.
   1951 *Client-Centered Therapy.* Boston: Houghton Mifflin.
   1958 "The Characteristics of a Helping Relationship," *Personnel and Guidance Journal,* 37:6-16
   1961 *On Becoming a Person.* Boston: Houghton Mifflin.
   1967 "The Therapeutic Relationship: Recent Theory and Research." In C. H. Patterson, *The Counselor in the School: Selected Readings.* New York: McGraw-Hill, pp. 228-240.
   1975 "Empathic: An Unappreciated Way of Being," *The Counseling Psychologist,* 5:2, pp. 2-10.

Shertzer, Bruce, and Stone, Shelley C.
   1968 *Fundamentals of Counseling.* Boston: Houghton Mifflin.

Truax, Charles B., and Carkhuff, Robert R.
   1967 *Toward Effective Counseling and Psychotherapy: Training and Practice.* Chicago: Aldine.

Van Hoose, William H.
   1966 "Counseling With Children." *American Educational Research Association Abstracts.*

Van Hoose, William H., and Pietrofesa, John J.
   1970 *Counseling and Guidance in the Twentieth Century.* Boston: Houghton Mifflin.

Chapter 4 The Process of Counseling

Counseling may take place in formal or in informal ways and in one or more settings. Generally, however, counseling is carried on over a period of time—weeks, months, or even years. Regardless of the setting or the time sequence, there are some elements that are fundamental to the process. These elements are briefly described in the following section.

ELEMENTS IN THE PROCESS

Counselor Expertise The in-counseling behavior of the counselor is of primary importance. When the counselor agrees to provide help, he/she also agrees to commit energies and abilities to assist the counselee to change. He/She becomes a special person in the life of the counselee and is thus intervening in the life-space of another human being. Such counselor attitudes as acceptance, respect, and trust have already been discussed; however, it needs to be emphasized again that these elements are crucial to effective counseling.

Additionally, when a counselor agrees to assist a client, he/she assumes the role of an expert, an authority, at least in the perception of society. The counselor's "authority comes from the fact that he/she has been extensively trained and has received disciplined exposure to the systematic theory and accumulated knowledge in the field, that he/she has developed appropriate and effective occupational behaviors and practiced these burgeoning skills under the watchful eye and shaping hand of qualified supervisors, that, in brief, he/she knows what to do and when to do it because he/she has been schooled and certified by experts. Thus, acquired authority, the result of concentrated study and training, distinguishes the professional from the layman whose chief difference lies in his/her comparative ignorance in the given area of occupational specialization (Pietrofesa and Vriend, 1971). Whatever the counselor's own feelings, he/she must accept this role and should do so with the full knowledge of psychological consequences to both the client and the counselor. The background and training of counselors vary a great deal. The effective counselor will, of course, recognize his/her limitations and, if necessary, will so advise the counselee, or he/she may make a referral to a more appropriate helper.

Counselor Skill The skill of the counselor is a second critical element in the counseling process. Following a request for help or a referral from another person such as a teacher or parent, the counselor makes some tentative assessment of the situation including whether he/she can or should help the client. The accuracy of this initial assessment and judgments made in subsequent contacts with the client will be only as valid as the counselor's professional skill permits. The counselor, regardless of philosophical orientation, in large measure determines the method of help, the extent of intervention, the role of the counselor, and the role of the counselee in the counseling process. The counselor needs to assume facilitative responsibility. As counseling progresses, the counselor must continuously reassess, interpret, modify methods, and develop a plan of action with the counselee. This partly depends on the counselee's willingness to assume responsibility during counseling.

> It seems to us that the client who is given either too much responsibility or too little—for him—is going to find therapy a most frustrating and perhaps completely unrewarding experience. While the degree of responsibility the client is able to assume does not serve as a basis from which to prescribe a specific treatment, it does begin to provide indications as to the direction therapy might take. It also provides a basis for varying approaches within the treatment of any one client, depending on the amount of change in responsibility the client is able to assume. In other words, as the client grows or changes, treatment must change accordingly. [Pierce and Schauble, 1969, p. 76]

The quality of the efforts and the outcome of counseling will hinge upon the skill and expertise of the counselor. But counseling also involves "skill" in a reciprocal fashion. First, "the helper is a skilled person" who lives in an effective fashion and, second, "the client learns the skills he needs to live more effectively through the counseling process" (Egan, 1975, p. 19).

Counselor Values The values of the counselor will reflect themselves in the helping process. Counseling should aid clients in answering such questions as "Who am I?" "What can I be?" "How do I face life?" Such questions can be dealt with best in a nonjudgmental relationship. Yet the counselor is not without values; he/she has beliefs, attitudes, and biases, and cannot leave these aspects of self in the outer office while he/she counsels. But the counselor can be nonevaluative in relationships with clients and can refrain from imposing rigid standards upon others. As Arbuckle (1970b) notes, "The counselor can be open, flexible, and not bound by any dogma, religious or secular, professional or personal" (p. 26).

This need for openness and flexibility in counselor value structure is crucial. The counselor cannot be defensive about values. Defensiveness consumes energy better spent elsewhere in the helping relationship. Such defensiveness is a reflection of the uncertainty felt about personal values—an uncertainty so great that no one had better question these values. Defensiveness about values really becomes a handicap for it limits areas that the counselor will be willing to explore.

The counselor who imposes his/her own values upon the counselee says essentially that the counselee is not as good as the counselor. At the same time he/she is saying, "I cannot trust you to make your own choices, so I must make them for you." A superior-inferior relationship is established. This is quite easy to do in light of suppositions brought to counseling by both the client and counselor. Jorgenson and Hurst (1972) found that the client sees the therapist as capable of healthier functioning than him/herself, while the therapist sees him/herself functioning more effectively than the client.

The counselor must be open and flexible enough not to allow this to happen. The counselor by simply admonishing the counselee will not change a thing. Instead he/she will jeopardize the relationship by creating guilt and resentment against him/herself.

The counselor needs to be comfortable about personal values for they are conceptual guidelines—guidelines into which specific behaviors and actions may fall for the client and even the counselor. In other words choices, decisions, and behaviors of the client are reflections of a value structure. Therapeutic behaviors of the counselor also are within the context of a value structure. A counselor who is uncomfortable about values will be unnecessarily constrictive of client freedom and quite restrictive of his/her own professional behavior. The counselor needs to allow for an open examination of personal values at all times for with such examination comes increased growth and competence. The real challenge today is no longer one of whether or not to impose values upon the client but the dilemma of "how to deal with our own values while permitting the other person the freedom to act on their own values" (Goodstein, 1973, p. 64).

At times the counselee will demonstrate an interest in the counselor's own values. He/She might ask, "What do you think?" The counselor must be sensitive to the real meaning of such a question. For example, the counselee might be searching for support. The counselor should then respond to the basic intent. On the other hand, there are times when the counselor would be less then authentic if he/she does not answer a question which demonstrates genuine interest in the counselor's values. It is acceptable in such circumstances for the counselor to be quite open. He/She already displays some values by wearing certain clothes and by working in a particular setting. He/She can, if necessary, state first, "This is how I feel, and it is quite all right for us to have different views." The overriding factor, once again, is that *the counselor does not impose his/her values upon the counselee.*

Counselor Responsibility to the Counselee The counselor must consider the fact that each individual is attempting to satisfy his/her own viscerogenic and psychogenic needs, while concurrently fulfilling obligations to the larger society. Sometimes a person's needs and his/her moral responsibilities for society's survival correspond, but at times they do not. What implications and ramifications does the latter instance contain for the counselor? Assuming the outcome of the counselee's choice does not violate or harm another, should the counselor help the counselee gratify his/her own needs or should the counselor see to it that the counselee's obligations to society be discharged? (Since most individuals have a need to become an accepted and respected member of a functioning group, the counselee's achievement of a compromise of his/her needs and the society's aims is not as difficult as it might appear.) Dimick and Huff (1970) contend that:

> Many practicing counselors have tended to function only as agents of socialization, conformity, and 'averageness.' They have tended to make or help the child 'fit' his environment rather than to help him transcend and change it. They have tended to support the establishment which stifles and constricts man's inherent potentials rather than challenging and working to effect societal changes which can aid in man's liberation. [p. 113]

A prime consideration within the counselor-counselee relationship is that the former has a responsibility to respect the decisions of the latter once they are formulated. If these decisions are finalized and are supportive of one's societal obligation to become a fully functioning person within the laws of that culture, all well and good. The counselor, however, must be willing to accept a counselee's decision that the counselor, as a citizen, might frown upon, e.g., smoking pot, or withdrawing from school to enter the armed forces. The counselor should not try to fit the counselee into the accepted social or school pattern by attempting to dissuade him/her from any decision

There are a great number of socializing agencies which attempt to shape the individual during growth so that his/her behavior fits the acceptable social pattern. At times these institutions, such as the school, church, family, and government, become so powerful that they engender conformity for its own sake. Counselees may rebel against this overconformity, which is stifling and inhibitive, and counselors must respect their decisions to do so.

The school, as mentioned previously, is a major social institution. The school in America, while trying to socialize the pupil, also is given the task of helping children learn how to make choices for themselves. The school counselor's primary function should be to help the counselee to help him/herself rather than to shape the individual according to a preconceived mold. The school situation generally lends itself to socialization responsibilities. Somewhere within that institution there must be a haven where each child can consider his/her own needs rather than the needs of society.

Socializing institutions have as one of their prime functions the 'housebreaking' of the people served. But the counselor serving in these institutions has as one of his prime functions the liberation of clients from restrictions not functional to their optimum development. How is this paradox handled? Often by distorting the purpose of counseling. The counselor is seen by the institution employing him as an ally who helps make people 'good.' But his unique task is not to make people 'good," but rather to make them 'real.' 'Real' in the sense that they assume responsibility for their actions, examine and act on their values, acquire their beliefs by thought and feeling and not by inheritance, and bravely come to terms with society not by surrender but by mutual accommodation. When 'real' they may or may not seem 'good' in the eyes of the socializing institutions, which by definition will be conservative as their function is to induce the individual into the world that is. [Steffire, 1970, p. 257]

The authentic counselor will be a self-actualizing person. (See Chapter 7). He/She will value personal freedom and personal choice but will have no need to impose these values on others. He/She may serve as a model, not only to be imitated, but as a source from which counselees can draw strength and thus gradually become capable of experiencing a high level of personal freedom (Arbuckle, 1970b, p. 27). Arbuckle (1970a) sums it up well:

> It would seem that there is a place in the school system for a professionally competent individual who, like the private psychotherapist, is there for the well-being of the individual, not the system. Teachers and administrators tend to represent the value system of the society of which the school is an arm, and these values mean little to a significant and growing portion of the young today. The counselor should be the one person in the school who has at least some chance of bridging the gap between the youth culture and the adult culture, so that each may come to feel a real need for each other. The counselor is not the enemy of the system, but he is for the individual. [p. 329]

Counseling—An Active Process Counseling, particularly in educational settings, cannot be a passive process. One of the participants must assume primary responsibility for setting the process in motion and for determining the method and direction of counseling. In schools, as a result of the societal view of the adult as the tutor and the client as the student, the counselor is thrust into the role of assuming responsibility for the client, whether he/she likes it or not. It is our view that such a posture is not inconsistent with such necessary counselor behaviors as openness, flexibility, acceptance, and nonevaluation. Put another way, the counselor can permit a client to experience a nonthreatening, deep, and secure relationship through counseling while at the same time providing some anchor points from which the counselee can develop a personal way of coping and experiencing.

Thus an important aspect of the counseling process involves the development of responsibility of roles of counselor and counselee. Initially, the counselor may assume primary responsibility. He/She helps the client move to a position of sharing responsibility, and finally, if counseling is effective, the client begins to make separate choices, plans, and decisions. Traxler (1970) writes:

> Both counselee and counselor should participate in reaching decisions pertinent to the counselee's welfare...The point of view taken there is that the final decision on any

problem is the counselee's responsibility and that he should take the lead in arriving at the decision, but that the counselor, out of his greater experience, should volunteer information and suggest and clarify alternatives to assist the counselee in his decision making. The giving of information and the making of tentative suggestions should not be allowed to become disguised coercion through which the counselor actually becomes the decision maker. [pp. 287-288]

To denote counseling as "an active process" means more than simply respecting the decisions of the client. It indicates that the counselor is giving the self—is one with the counselee—during the process. There is a commitment established to help the counselee to become self-actualizing. With this in mind, how active does the counselor become? Does he/she go out and find the client a job? The counselor operates in most cases on propositions such as (1) not making the counselee dependent upon him/her and (2) helping the counselee achieve control of his/her own destiny. It is likely then that the counselee needs a relationship established where he/she can think through courses of action and subsequently plan to implement and, possibly, reevaluate them.

Sometimes more may be necessary if the counselor is really committed to the fulfillment of human potential. He/She may have to become active outside the confines of the counseling endeavor. This may be the case in helping elementary school age youth. Dimick and Huff (1970) point this out.

> Most certainly, children are not as free as adults to unilaterally choose those ways of living which would be most enhancing to them. They do live in a more controlling environment where adult expectations for children are well defined; hence, the role of the counselor is to help the child live more fully through direct and indirect means. Directly, he can aid children in the evolution of attitudes and behaviors which promote growth toward their optimal functioning levels. Indirectly, he can help those adults who control the child's world to modify their attitudes and behaviors so that the environment of the child allows for the realization of his potentials. [pp. 113-114]

If the environment cannot be changed, the counselor must concentrate on the child's perception of circumstances.

Counselor Behavior—Counselee Resistance The counselor should be able to prevent the development of counselee resistance. The counselor, who is secure, has satisfying relations with others while his/her insecure counterpart is preoccupied with preserving self. In an increasingly depersonalized society, preserving behavior rather than growth behavior is prevalent.

Counselee reactions which preserve the self—negative or self-destructive—may be much more complex than the counselor imagines. Laing (1960) in *The Divided Self* has given new insight into possible counselee reactions to the counseling situation. The student, for example, who comes to the school counselor, sees the counselor as another agent of the school and, therefore, may try to prevent the self from being known. This is a defensive posture, for if one is not truly involved then one cannot be hurt. The maneuver becomes one of isolation or withdrawal to preserve identity. The counselee with low grades might state, "I don't know why" or "I'll try to do better." Another type of resistance might find the counselee disassociating himself from his/her true feelings and beliefs and assuming a role he/she thinks the counselor would approve.

Counselee resistance to cooperation in the counseling endeavor may be a natural outgrowth of the client's ambivalence about growth and change. Phenomenologically, the consistency of current behavior, while perhaps uncomfortable, offers security while behavior change, even though it may appear attractive, might make the client unsure and provoke anxiety. Most people are being pulled concurrently by behavior maintenance and behavior growth forces. Facilitative conditions provide the security necessary under which change will occur.

There are many indications of counselee resistance. Such indications might range from the obvious—missing or being late for appointments, questioning the value of counseling, or terminating the counseling sessions—to the less obvious—emphasizing the cognitive rather than the affective, the past rather than the present, and the non-self (e.g., other people) rather than the self. Resorting to silence or short, brusque comments is probably the most common type of resistance. Brammer and Shostrom (1968) describe five levels of symptom intensity.

At the *lagging* level, the client shuns responsibility to the counselor, is sluggish in response, distractible, and concerned with intellectualization rather than emotional content ...

The *inertia* level contains more pronounced disinterest manifested by short answers, disregard of counselor leads, and fatigue.

Tentative resistance includes indications that the client is unwilling to continue the interview. Some indications are: arguing, excessive qualifying, showing physical tension, and inhibiting expression of hostility, anxiety, and guilt feelings.

True resistance is described as an intensification of the tentative type ... such as ... remaining silent ..., questioning the competence of the counselor, or using vituperative language.

The most extreme form ... is described as *rejection*. The forms are generally extreme, such as terminating the interview by flat request, making hostile remarks about the counselor .... [p. 261]

Regardless of its manifest symptoms, resistance is essentially a drawing in, the raising of a protective shield, and a denial, at least for the time being, of growth forces. Following are three short illustrations of counselee resistance.

DIALOGUE 1 The first dialogue involves client resistance reflected by abrupt answers and unwillingness to disclose self to the counselor. The counselee (nine-year-old girl) is in the throes of a parental divorce.

Counselor: Hi, Renee, how have you been?
Client: Fine.
Counselor: I was worried that you might miss this week because of swimming.
Client: I'm going from here to swimming.
Counselor: You're going swimming after you're done down here today?
Client: Yeah. [*Silence, five seconds*]
Counselor: You're going to get to do both then, huh?
Client: Yeah. [*Silence, three seconds*]

Counselor: Well, how have you been this week?
Client: Fine.
Counselor: Are you enjoying this warm weather now?
Client: Yeah!
Counselor: This would be a perfect day to go swimming.
Client: Yeah.
Counselor: I bet you are looking forward to that aren't you?
Client: Yeah.
Counselor: That will be good. [*Silence, six seconds*] We talked quite a bit last week, Renee . . . and a . . . I really enjoyed it last week. Do you know why I enjoyed it so much?
Client: No.
Counselor: Because you were talking to me about a lot of things that you liked. You told me about how you feel about certain things. That was enjoyable . . . Do you like talking with people?
Client: Not that much.
Counselor: Not that much . . . huh . . . well that's ok.
Client: [Quickly] Yeah!
Counselor: You still do?
Client: Yep!!
Counselor: Today I saw you in the lobby—what in the world were you doing out there when I came over?
Client: I was playing in the showcase.
Counselor: I looked up and I thought I saw a little girl in the showcase. I said to myself . . . I know that little girl. How did you get up there? Did you jump up by yourself?
Client: Yeah.
Counselor: Did you know who those other children were that were in there with you?
Client: Yeah, Frankie and my sister.
Counselor: How about that big girl . . . who was that big girl?
Client: I don't know. [Silence]

Counselor: You like to play like that!
Client: Yeah.
Counselor: Would you like to tell me about anything that you have on your mind?
Client: No.
Counselor: No . . . you wouldn't?
Client: No.
Counselor: Why don't you? [Silence]
Client: I don't know.
Counselor: Uh, huh.
Client: I hardly have anything to say today.
Counselor: Hardly anything at all?
Client: No.
Counselor: Why don't you tell me something about school?
Client: We had a substitute today, again.
Counselor: Which teacher was that for?
Client: At school.
Counselor: Was it your homeroom teacher who was absent?
Client: Yes.
Counselor: How did you feel about that?
Client: When she told us Monday . . . we all said ah,ah,ah, because she has been out last Tuesday and Friday, and she's going to be out next Tuesday and Friday, too.
Counselor: She told you in advance that she was going to be absent?
Client: Yeah . . . because of her teeth.
Counselor: Her teeth are bothering her again.
Client: When we have a sub we always run around the room.
Counselor: It's a new teacher that just comes in?
Client: Yeah, my teacher asks them if they want to come in and be the teacher just for the day.
Counselor: I'm not sure I understand. Is it a woman or a man?
Client: Yeah, not a man.

84 The Authentic Counselor

Counselor: Oh.
Client: The boys want a man teacher; the girls want a woman teacher. There's only twelve boys and twenty-two girls.
Counselor: Girls like to have a woman teacher and the boys like to have a man teacher.
Client: Yeah ... there's only thirty-four in our room. [Silence, six seconds]
Counselor: Which do you prefer to have?
Client: Women.
Counselor: What do you like best about women teachers?
Client: I don't know.
Counselor: Do you have any male teachers in your school?
Client: In our school there are two men.
Counselor: There are two men teachers in your school?
Client: Yeah, they teach fifth and sixth graders.
Counselor: So you haven't had them yet.
Client: No.
Counselor: Do you think you will like it if you have a man teacher?
Client: Yeah.
Counselor Have you thought about ... [Notice the abrupt answer before the question is even completed]
Client: No.
Counselor: I know that when my little boy comes home sometimes he tells me that when they get a substitute ... that sometimes if a man comes in—my boy has a woman teacher—that the man comes in and he talks louder and sometimes the kids get a little upset when they hear a man's voice because he talks so deep. Sometimes he yells out 'All right chidren' and everyone gets all upset. Does that bother you if somebody yells at you?
Client: Yeah.

Counselor: You mentioned that your dad has never talked loud to you.
Client: No.
Counselor: Does your mother?
Client: Yeah.
Counselor: Sometimes she does?
Client: Yeah.
Counselor: What makes your mother talk loud?
Client: When my brother starts yelling.
Counselor: What does your mother say to him?
Client: "Go to bed or sit on the couch until you stop crying."
Counselor: Tell me more about it.
Client: No.
Counselor: Does that upset you when someone cries?
Client: Yeah. [Yawn]
Counselor: Are you sleepy?
Client: [Nods head]
Counselor: It is kind of tiring today. [Silence] Did you get to bed early last night?
Client: No.
Counsleor: What happened last night?
Client: Had to take a bath, wash our hair and set it.
Counselor: Had to wash and set your hair last night?
Client: [Nods]
Counselor: Did you get to bed at your regular time or were you a little late?
Client: No, we were supposed to go to bed at 8:00 but we got to go to bed at 9:00.
Counselor: That's an hour later, huh?
Client: Yeah.

DIALOGUE 2 In this instance the client (a seventeen-year-old boy) terminates counseling after three sessions. Basically, he had identified his problem as being too dependent on his parents. Ironically, he feels he has handled his problem as a result of counseling, but he is terminating counseling because his parents do not approve of it.

Counselor: How are you today?

Client: Oh, fine.
Counselor: You're looking very happy.
Client: Yeah. I guess I am. [Laugh] Oh, well, I'll get right down to it.
Counselor: Yes, I'm looking forward to it.
Client: Ok. All right. I got home yes ... this is Monday night ...
Counselor: Uh, huh.
Client: I got home and the front door is open and my mother is cleaning the window. I said, "Ah ho! Here we go!" I walked into the house. And my, my father's in the den thumbing through a book, while he's watching T.V. I know that he doesn't do this normally so I guess that this is kind of a pretense. My mother doesn't look particularly happy, you know, she's a little sad. I walked to the kitchen. "Hi, Mom, how are you?" She said, "Fine. How did things go?" I said, "Went down and I got counseled." "Well, I didn't know you were going down?" And I said, "I told you I had problems," She goes, "Well, if you, if you had problems I would have paid, I would have got, you know, Dr. Heath; I would have got you counseling from him." She's going on like this and I go, "Well, Ma, I told you this." She goes, "Why didn't you tell me about this." She said, "You got a good home, What more do you want?" I said, "You don't understand me." So we're going to it and my father here is in the den and I *know* he's listening...
Counselor: Uh, huh. Did your father say much?
Client: Well, you know I said, "Hello Dad, how are you?" He said, "How are you, son?" I'd do something for him and he'd say, "Thank you." I made my needs felt and I did accomplish this much. Cause, you know, he doesn't really, he doesn't want to tangle with me and, ah, Ma says, "Well ... you know they're brainwashing you

down at ———." "Mom, all they do is *listen* to my problems . . . they just *listen* to me." She says, "I, I want you to stop this." So, I, figure here I have a bartering point, you see. I can, well, I can do this, but I can get this for it, too. So, um, I don't know. I think I've kind of compromised with my parents. I think this will be my last time down here at ———.
Counselor: Oh.
Client: And, well, I've done another thing for you. I've got you a real nut! He . . . [Laugh] I've got myself a replacement.
Counselor: Fine.
Client: . . . you'll find him an interesting person. A little background on him [Laugh] if you want it right now. He's rather a short, overweight fellow. He is sensitive. He's got a stepfather. I don't think that this stepfather really has ever been hard on him. But his early childhood, I think he kept moving around a lot.
Counselor: Uh, huh.
Client: And he never really got established anywhere. I think to some extent he does use dexadrine.
Counselor: Um.
Client: You know, speed. Once in a while he will. He just seems to get strung out.
Counselor: Right.
Client: But he seems to *stay* that way.
Counselor: And he's going to be taking your place.
Client: Yeah.
Counselor: Uh, um.
Client: I told him, "I'm gonna quit, you know, and you can take my place." He goes, "Yeah." [Laugh]
Counselor: Was this, then, a bartering point?
Client: It was a bartering point for me, yes.
Counselor: And you think you've achieved total independence now?
Client: I've achieved . . . a great deal. . .

Counselor: ... a great deal ...
Client: Great deal, yeah.

DIALOGUE 3 Following is an excerpt in which the counselee keeps the focus on the counselor.

Counselor: Do you enjoy doing things for your mother?
Client: Yeah, but I stopped doing that now.
Counselor: Why?
Client: I don't know. I go to school and my mom doesn't want me to be late. I get up on time and then fool around. [Giggle] I wanna ask you somethin'.
Counselor: What would you like to ask me?
Client: I wanna ask you ... Do you know why your husband wanted to marry you?
Counselor: Why my husband wanted to marry me? I think so.
Client: Why?
Counselor: Well, because he loves me and [Giggle from Carol] ... Is that funny?
Client: I don't know.
Counselor: Does it bother you when I use the word love?
Client: I don't know. Uh, uh ... that doesn't bother me. I just like to hear sometimes from you.
Counselor: You like to hear about me?
Client: How come he loves you?
Counselor: That's a good question. It's hard for me to answer.
Client: [Giggle] I wonder why you said you wanted some kids. I think I know why. Because you wanna give them lickins.
Counselor: Is that what mothers are for? To spank?
Client: Is that woman counselor with Stefanie married?
Counselor: No, but she's getting married soon. How do you feel about people getting married?
Client: It's ok. I wanna see your husband sometime. I wanna ask him somethin'.

Counselor: Can you ask me?
Client: Yeah—but I wanna see what he says. 'Cause you're not for sure.
Counselor: About what?
Client: Why he married you.
Counselor: Why do people get married?
Client: I don't know—because they love each other I guess.
Counselor: Do you know what love is?
Client: Uh, um. Like you like somebody a whole bunch.
Counselor: How do you feel about a person you love.
Client: I feel ok. I wanna ask you somethin'. I don't know whether it's important or not. Did you and your husband ever have fights? You know ... fusses?
Counselor: Once in a while.
Client: [*Laugh*] What do you all fuss about?
Counselor: What do we fuss about? We don't have many arguments. I don't see him too often to fight a lot.
Client: Why did you all get married if you don't see him much?
Counselor: We're both pretty busy now. Do you think it's important to spend time with people that you love and like?
Client: Don't you?
Counselor: Of course. I'd like to. But sometimes you can't.
Client: I just wanna ask him to see what he says.
Counselor: About why he married me? Why do you think he did?
Client: Because he loved you. And he asked you if you'd marry him. I asked my teacher 'cause she's kinda cute, if anybody asked her to marry her.
Counselor: Your teacher's not married?
Client: No. My teacher's a nun!

The counselor's reaction to the resistant counselee is crucial. Most important, he/she must accept rather then become threatened by such resistance. It is quite understandable how a counselor in practicum, under the watchful eyes of a supervisor, however benevolent, and several peers, can have his/her security jeopardized. More than once we have heard the expression, "The little bastard won't cooperate." While this statement gives an indication of possible client resistance, it more appropriately describes the hostility the counselor feels toward the counselee. The counselor at such a time needs to look at why he/she is so anxious and possibly hostile, and take appropriate action. Colleagues and supervisors can offer helpful suggestions, e.g., a change in technique, possible use of play media with small children, etc.

What, more specifically, can the counselor do upon encountering resistance?

> Confronted with 'patient resistance' we should immediately consider alternate explanations that could account for the patient's unwillingness to accept the therapist's message. Perhaps poor cognitive ability on the part of the patient prevents him from grasping the full intent of the therapist's remarks, or the frame of reference used by the therapist may be so discrepant from that used by the patient that the very meaning of words is not the same for both. Finally, the manner in which the therapist presents his comments may blind the patient from understanding his full intent. [Goldstein et. al., 1966, pp. 147-148]

The counselor can follow several basic procedures upon encountering resistance.

1. Accept the responsibility for helping the counselee recognize and deal with any resistance. It is necessary that the client accept the responsibility for his/her nongrowth behavior.
2. Continue to provide a therapeutic atmosphere characterized by warmth, understanding, acceptance, and genuineness.
3. Do not bring forth highly threatening material which would only increase the counselee's resistance. Similarly, it is probably best not to resort to interpretation which (a) may be seen as counselee-attacking behavior, or (b) may encourage the counselee to intellectualize. Both may intensify the resistance.
4. Emphasize the "feeling" level of any counselee response, rather than simple content. This is one way certainly for the counselor to convey a willingness to understand.

5. Give the counselee an opportunity to take the lead. The counselor might maintain an "interested silence" as long as it does not in itself become threatening. In a recent observation, one practicum counselor was threatened by his counselee's short answers. Upon timing his questions, he found that less than two seconds elapsed between each. He gave the counselee little opportunity to assume the lead. Finally, when the nine-year-old child did start to say more than one word, the counselor interrupted her.

The preceding are simply suggestions and are not meant to be prescriptive, for as Blocher (1966) points out:

> There are no general pat solutions or techniques that will solve relationship problems. The best approach to most of these relationship phenomena is one of direct, open, and honest reaction to the client. If the counselor can be secure enough to deal with the relationship in these ways, some of this security will usually be communicated to the client and will help him be more open, trusting, and confident. [p. 153]

ESTABLISHING SECURITY The establishment of security becomes a necessary prerequisite to inducing nondefensive and growth-producing behavior in the counselee. The following excerpt of a counseling dialogue involves a neophyte counselor-trainee in his first interview. The counselor is able to provide the security necessary so that the counselee does not feel threatened. In addition he is able to establish a good relationship with the counselee. He does not impose his values upon the counselee and, although at times she becomes defensive, does a more than adequate job in trying to help her understand her attitudes and feelings.

Counselor: What brought you down to the counseling center?
Client: Mainly it's my mom who told me to come down. And my counselor at school, he thought I should come, too. So I thought I would come down so that I would keep her, that is, my mother, you know . . .
Counselor: So that you can keep your mother happy?

Client: Yeah.

Counselor: You were saying that you didn't particularly want to come.

Client: No, really, Oh, I don't know. I don't really know. I can't . . .

Counselor: You were saying something about troubles. Tell me a little bit more about what you mean by these troubles.

Client: Well, I've been going to school and I've been skipping. My mom found out and she didn't know why and so that bothers her. She doesn't like the way I act. And she thinks I'm crazy or something.

Counselor: How do you feel about that?

Client: Well, I suppose I act crazy around her?

Counselor: You mean around your mother?

Client: Yeah, Well, like, she thinks I'm crazy because I say things that aggravate her and she doesn't understand that. She doesn't understand why I'm saying it.

Counselor: The things that you say to her?

Client: Yeah. Because they aggravate her.

Counselor: Can you tell me more about some of these things, that is, because I really don't have a clear picture?

Client: Yeah, I know. Let's see. Well, I don't know. You know, just little things. Like any situation that will come up she'll want to ask where are you going? And I'll say I don't know. So she gets all upset, but I've told her four times. I tell her to calm down when I tell her I'm going out. She asks me about ten times—no, not really ten times, but you know she seems like she's asking . . .

Counselor: She keeps asking often enough.

Client: And that bothers me. So I can be very sarcastic, and that aggravates her. I know it aggravates her and I keep on doing it because I want her to see how it makes me feel. But she doesn't see that. She might see it for just a moment. The next time she'll do the same thing. I realize that it's just her personality.

Counselor: You . . .

Client: And that's how she is, but, I, oh, I don't know. It's just me.

Counselor: You aggravate her because you want to make her understand how you feel. Does that mean that you feel that way too?

Client: Well, no, it's not that I intentionally do it. Well, sometimes I do. Sometimes I know when she'll be mad, but I'll say it anyway.

Counselor: You want to make her mad.

Client: It's just that I meant to make her see why I'm feeling this way. Sometimes she'll say something and I'll just go along with her, to make her happy. And other times I won't. I'll say what I really think and I know it will be aggravating to her. I do it anyway to make her understand how I really am, but she doesn't see that. She says, "You must stay awake just thinking up those things. You must sit up nights trying to figure out ways to make me mad or to make me feel bad." You know, and really I don't.

Counselor: Well, sometimes you deliberately do it and sometimes . . .

Client: And sometimes I don't. I don't really deliberately do it, but sometimes I'm my real self. I say what I mean although I know it'll make her mad. Sometimes I'll just fake it and be like what she wants me to be and just go along with her.

Counselor: You mention this real self and I really don't know what it is.

Client: O.K. She wanted me to go to Florida over Easter. I didn't particularly want to go because two years ago I went and we stayed at my aunt's on the Gulf. I had a nice time, but there were a lot of things happening over Easter. I met a whole bunch of new people since I've been going to high school, and different things were going on. So I practically didn't care if I had gone or not, for all I would be doing there will be lying on the sand getting tanned for awhile ... Sounds rough? Nothing spectacular, and I really didn't care if I went or not. She wanted me to go. It bothered her that I didn't so I just said O.K., I'll go! And on the coast I had fun but ...

Counselor: You preferred to stay home with your new friends.

Client: Yeah! My girl friend came with me, and so we had a good time, but it didn't matter to me if I went or not. In fact, I sort of at the beginning ... I would rather have stayed home.

Counselor: It seems one thing that is the real self is that you would like more time away from your mother. You have the feeling that you have to do a lot of things with her.

Client: Yeah! I really don't want to be around her at all. I mean that's another problem, because I keep telling her that I'm going to leave and I can't wait till I do. That bothers her because, you know, she keeps saying what's wrong around here. I'm the only one that's really home now. Chris just graduated from college so she'll be home until August when she'll get married. Diana left and so did Paul. Now Chris; then I'm the youngest.

Counselor: I'm not sure, but it seems that you're not really that upset about leaving.

Client: I feel sorry for my mom. She's all by herself and she really shouldn't be. It's really weird because she started dating again. I just can't believe it. It's like being a mother with a child who is just starting to date, watching them, being excited about their dates and her telling her girl friends about it. She'll go out with some guy. Then on the phone she is talking to a woman in her office, I mean just for some business reason or something. She's good friends with her and she'll just call her up because she just can't wait to tell her. It's really strange. She needs people around her. But I feel sorry for her because I can see how it must be like.

Counselor: You understand because you feel that way, too.

Client: Well, you know, sometimes I tell her that I really hate her. I mean I don't hate her. It's just that I'm trying to impress upon her ... No, I don't hate her at all. It's just the fact that I'm trying to impress the fact that I really don't need her that much for her maternal love. I know that she is still trying to be like a mother is to a daughter. Sometimes she'll gesture like trying to fondle you or something like that. I think it's hard for her to accept the fact that I'm getting older.

Counselor: Um humm. You object to the fact that she treats you younger than you really are.

Client: Well, I don't really see her that much ...

Counselor: It seems that there are a lot of things your mother does that annoy you. [Laugh].

Client: [Laugh] Yeah, I know. Everything.

Counselor: I was kind of wondering what are your feelings about the whole thing, about the relationship?

Client: [Nervous laugh]

Counselor: You say you hate her and then you really don't hate her.

Client: O.K. Like I really don't hate her. I say that just to impress upon her that I don't need her.

Counselor: You really want her to pay attention to you, then.

Client: I want her to see why I'm doing this.

Counselor: That's where I get all mixed up.

Client: She doesn't like the way I act; she doesn't like the things I do. She doesn't like the way I talk to her and talk to my friends. Everything I do, she objects to it. Well, it's . . . [*She starts to get tears in her eyes*] [*A long pause*]

Counselor: You feel quite upset.

Client: Ah, I don't know. Let's see. [*Pause*] [*Spends the next several minutes talking about school*]

Counselor: It's just so frustrating for you. She doesn't understand the way you think and feel.

Client: I really don't care, really. She's not important to me, really. I don't think of her. I just think of her as a necessary thing. I really do. That makes me feel bad, too. You're always brought up with certain ideas, and how you love and respect this person and that person, and hate this person and that person. Anyhow, it seems that it's sort of drilled into you. She's always spouting this and that about her childhood. How she's brought up this way and that way. "How come you're not that way?" Well, I feel bad that things aren't the way she wants things to be. But I can't help the way I feel. So I just don't feel she's important at all.

Counselor: She doesn't understand you.

Client: No, because I've always been off, cut off from the rest of the family. I guess I've always been independent. I really wasn't an awful nice kid. There were kids across the street that I liked to play with and for a while there, I was playing with my brother and his friends. I was a real tomboy. Every time he got a black eye, I did. The kids across the street wouldn't run around as I did. Whenever I did things, they would want to do them, too, but I would get them into trouble because they weren't supposed to be doing this or that. I wouldn't get into trouble because my mother was never home. She didn't know anything about this. So the mothers of the other children would say they couldn't play with me. And so that really hurt me.

Counselor; You felt rejected.
Client: Yeah, I really did. I'd pretend it didn't really matter.
Counselor: But it did all the time.
Client: Yeah. Right! So, when my family was all at home in the evening, I'd try to get their attention. The children in the family would say, "Cut it out!" My brother, who's four years older than I, started to outgrow playing with me, and at times he just wanted me to go away.
Counselor: And again, you felt he was shooing you away.
Client: Yeah, right! My mom and dad felt sorry for me because I was left home all the time. Just Donald was playing with me. I ended up pretty spoiled.
Counselor: That isn't what you wanted. You didn't want them to feel sorry for you; you just wanted them to know you were there.
Client: Yeah. [*Starts to cry again, followed by two to three minutes of silence*] You know, I think I better go now. I'm, I'm feeling better.
Counselor: Would you like to come back?
Client: Yeah. That would be fine. Tomorrow, O.K.?
Counselor: Sure. Let's go make an appointment.

TRANSFERENCE During transference the client attaches to the counselor tendencies or characteristics which had previously been associated with another person. Concurrently, the psychological reactions which corresponded to the earlier perceptions are also displaced on the counselor. Transference often reflects the human being's tendency to classify another person and at the same time allow one to behave in a fashion which is familiar and hence comfortable.

Transferences can occur which are either negative or positive in nature. The former reflects counselee resentments or unfriendliness which results in a blocking of the therapeutic effort, while the latter is a display of warmth toward the counselor resulting in the counselee's being cooperative. Belkin (1975) points out that "whenever the counselor feels he is being perceived as if he were someone other than who he really is, it is reasonably certain that the transference is at work" (p. 210).

We have found that transference is likely to occur when the counselee feels dependent on the counselor. Perhaps this is one reason why the counselor should continue to emphasize counselee control of environment. One of the writers remembers a situation in which, as a school counselor, he became active in helping to find a talented student a scholarship to a nearby university. On several occasions, he actually drove the young lady for admission interviews. It soon became apparent in future counseling sessions that the counselor had assumed a fatherly image. (Her father had died when she was quite young.)

Several signs point to the development of transference:

1. The counselee displays likes or dislikes out of proportion to the situation.

2. The counselee may show too much interest in the counselor—or overemphasize a counselor trait. He/She may be overly concerned for the counselor's welfare.

3. The counselee may not be able to focus upon any concern. He/She may continually misunderstand what the counselor is saying.

4. The counselee may engage in attention-seeking behaviors, e.g., continual tardiness or illness.

The counselor accepts, clarifies, reflects and interprets as he/she would any other feelings in counseling, and in doing so will generally bring the counselee to the realization of what is going on, enabling him/her to cope with and accept the responsibility for the transference and break its dependency roots. This may be threatening, but ignoring these feelings "will not be a satisfactory solution for either counselor or client" (Blocher, 1966, p. 152). The process does serve a significant function, for "The awareness of freedom to express previously repressed irrational feelings is a unique experience which often reduces anxiety" (Brammer and Shostrom, 1968, p. 238).

STEPS IN THE COUNSELING PROCESS The counseling process, then, can be described as a continuous process of interaction between counselee and counselor. The process contains some dimensions that can be described and analyzed. Maier (1965, p. 222) presents a schematic diagram of the counseling process (Figure 5). Maier points to the importance, then, of diagnosis, not as a prelude to treatment, and treatment not as a terminal activity, but rather diagnosis and treatment as "continuously interwoven" throughout the helping process. Human discordance has many causes and requires both scientific and artistic know-how on the part of the counselor. The two processes, diagnosis and treatment, since they are continuously meshed, require constant feedback and ongoing reformulations as basic considerations are altered.

FIGURE 5. Steps in the Counseling Process
(Maier, 1965, p. 222)

HELPING PROCESS

DIAGNOSIS AND TREATMENT

Eight Steps of the Helping Process
1. Observing situation
2. Ordering and assessing observation
3. Predicting course of development **without** intervention
4. Predicting course of development **with** intervention
5. Formulating tentative hypothesis and alternate
6. Purposeful intervention, including acknowledged noninterference
7. Observing anew after intervention
8. Reassessing the previous appraisal and formulating new hypothesis

--- --- --- --- --- --- --- --- --- --- --- --- --- --- --- --- --- --- --- ---

Subdivisions of the Counseling Process

Study Process	*Appraisal Process*	*Treatment Process*
Observation (1)	Prediction without intervention (3)	Purposeful intervention (6)
Ordering and assessing the observations (2)	Prediction with intervention (4)	
Observing anew after intervention (7)	Formulation of a hypothesis (5)	
	Reassessing the previous appraisal and formulation of new hypothesis (8)	

The study processes focus upon observation, ordering, and assessing those observations and observing anew some sort of intervention. Dual concentration is upon both a problem and its circumstances. The counselee's world is important as are past experiences which are relevant to the present. The counselor, too, needs an ordering of data to make the process most meaningful to the client.

The appraisal process develops "applicable propositions" which evolved from the study process. Previous observations and classifications are useless if they are simply meant to be descriptive data; they become meaningful as a preparation for action.

Treatment can involve any number of therapeutic processes. It involves a "mobilization of interpersonal relationships and the skillful application of specific techniques" (Maier, 1965, p. 232). Treatment necessarily involves a helping relationship as a fundamental means—a vehicle—for change activities.

Another view of the process in a behavioral context is presented by Hendricks et al. (1973). Counseling variables are stated as specific "competencies" rather than vague generalities.

FIGURE 6

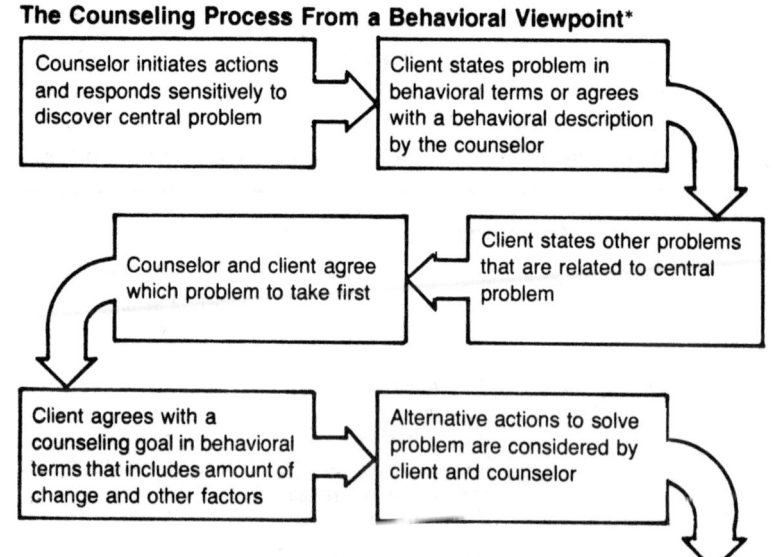

The Counseling Process From a Behavioral Viewpoint*

```
┌─────────────────────────┐      ┌─────────────────────────┐
│ Counselor initiates     │      │ Client states problem in│
│ actions and responds    │ ───▶ │ behavioral terms or     │
│ sensitively to discover │      │ agrees with a behavioral│
│ central problem         │      │ description by the      │
│                         │      │ counselor               │
└─────────────────────────┘      └─────────────────────────┘
                                              │
                                              ▼
      ┌─────────────────────────┐      ┌─────────────────────────┐
      │ Counselor and client    │      │ Client states other     │
      │ agree which problem     │ ◀─── │ problems that are       │
      │ to take first           │      │ related to central      │
      │                         │      │ problem                 │
      └─────────────────────────┘      └─────────────────────────┘
              │
              ▼
┌─────────────────────────┐      ┌─────────────────────────┐
│ Client agrees with a    │      │ Alternative actions to  │
│ counseling goal in      │      │ solve problem are       │
│ behavioral terms that   │ ───▶ │ considered by client    │
│ includes amount of      │      │ and counselor           │
│ change and other factors│      │                         │
└─────────────────────────┘      └─────────────────────────┘
                                              │
                                              ▼
```

The Process of Counseling

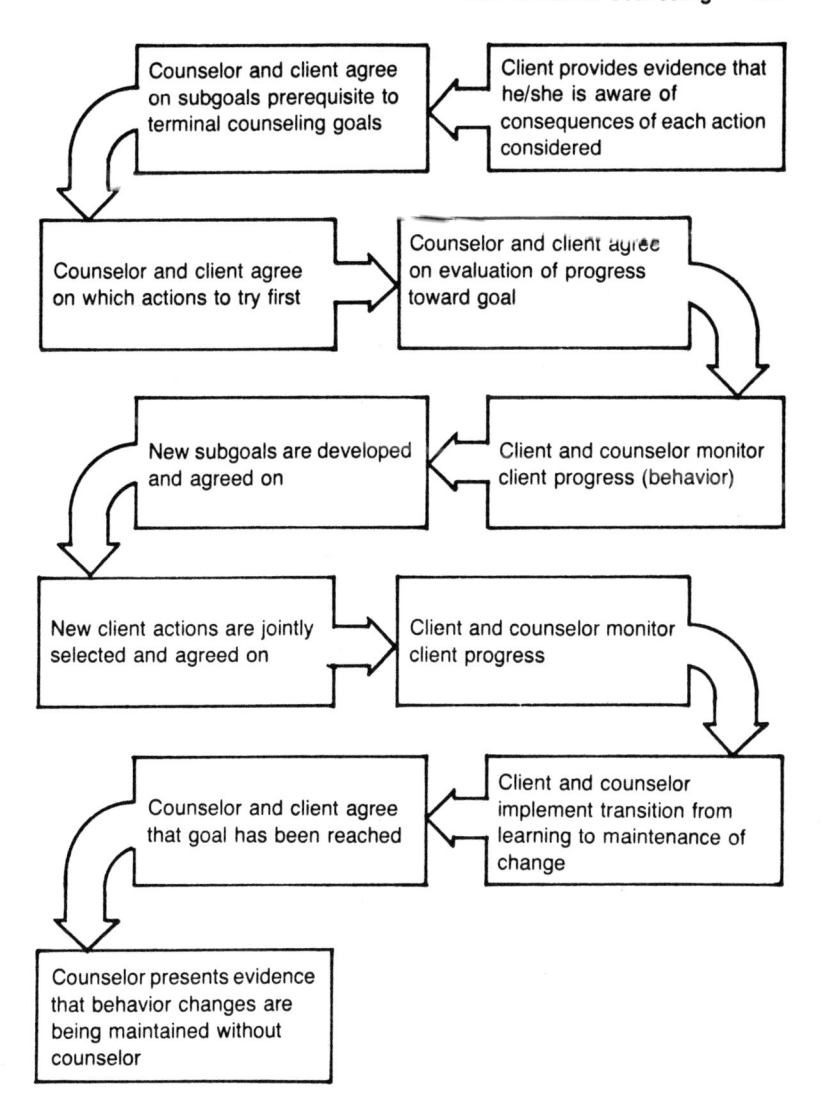

```
┌─────────────────────────────┐      ┌─────────────────────────────┐
│ Counselor and client agree  │ ←──  │ Client provides evidence    │
│ on subgoals prerequisite to │      │ that he/she is aware of     │
│ terminal counseling goals   │      │ consequences of each action │
└─────────────────────────────┘      │ considered                  │
         │                            └─────────────────────────────┘
         ▼
┌─────────────────────────────┐      ┌─────────────────────────────┐
│ Counselor and client agree  │ ──→  │ Counselor and client agree  │
│ on which actions to try     │      │ on evaluation of progress   │
│ first                       │      │ toward goal                 │
└─────────────────────────────┘      └─────────────────────────────┘
                                              │
                                              ▼
┌─────────────────────────────┐      ┌─────────────────────────────┐
│ New subgoals are developed  │ ←──  │ Client and counselor        │
│ and agreed on               │      │ monitor client progress     │
│                             │      │ (behavior)                  │
└─────────────────────────────┘      └─────────────────────────────┘
         │
         ▼
┌─────────────────────────────┐      ┌─────────────────────────────┐
│ New client actions are      │ ──→  │ Client and counselor        │
│ jointly selected and        │      │ monitor client progress     │
│ agreed on                   │      │                             │
└─────────────────────────────┘      └─────────────────────────────┘
                                              │
                                              ▼
┌─────────────────────────────┐      ┌─────────────────────────────┐
│ Counselor and client agree  │ ←──  │ Client and counselor        │
│ that goal has been reached  │      │ implement transition from   │
│                             │      │ learning to maintenance of  │
│                             │      │ change                      │
└─────────────────────────────┘      └─────────────────────────────┘
         │
         ▼
┌─────────────────────────────┐
│ Counselor presents evidence │
│ that behavior changes are   │
│ being maintained without    │
│ counselor                   │
└─────────────────────────────┘
```

Adapted from Hendricks, G. C., Ferguson, J. G., and Thorsen, C. E., "Toward Counseling Competencies: The Stanford Program," *Personnel and Guidance Journal*, 51 (1973):420.

SUMMARY

Counseling is a continual process whereby the counselor utilizes his/her expertise in facilitating decision making to assist the counselee to change. The counselor is a significant being in the life of the counselee. While the counselor certainly holds important values, he/she does not impose them on the counselee and certainly does not become an oppressive force for conformity. The counselor needs to be able to establish a counseling relationship with the counselee which induces growth rather than defensive or non-growth behavior.

REFERENCES

Arbuckle, D. S.
    1970a "Does the School Really Need Counselors?" *The School Counselor,* 17:325-330. Reprinted with permission of the publisher, American Personnel and Guidance Association, Washington, D.C.

    1970b "Theoretical and Philosophical Concepts." In W. Van Hoose, and J. J. Pietrofesa, *Counseling and Guidance in the Twentieth Century.* Boston: Houghton Mifflin, pp. 19-29.

Belkin, G.S.
    1975 *Practical Counseling in the Schools.* Dubuque, Iowa: W.C. Brown.

Blocher, D.H.
    1966 *Developmental Counseling.* New York: The Ronald Press. Copyright © The Ronald Press Company, New York.

Brammer, L.M., and Shostrom, E. L.
    1968 *Therapeutic Psychology,* rev. ed. Englewood Cliffs N.J.: Prentice Hall. By permission of the publisher.

Dimick, K. M., and Huff, V. E.
    1970 *Child Counseling.* Dubuque, Iowa; W. C. Brown.

Egan, G.
    1975 *The Skilled Helper.* Monterey California: Brooks/Cole.

Goldstein, A.P., Heller, K., and Seechrest, L.B.
    1966 *Psychotherapy and the Psychology of Behavior Change.* New York: Wiley.

Goodstein, Leonard D.
    1973 "The Place of Values in the World of Counseling." *Counseling Psychologist,* 4 (2), 63-66.

Hendricks, G.C., Ferguson, J. G., and Thorsen, C. E.
    1973 "Toward Counseling Competencies: The Stanford Program." *Personnel and Guidance Journal, 51,* p. 420.

Jorgenson, G.T. and Hurst, J.C.
 1972 "Empirical Investigation of Two Presuppositions in Counseling and Psychotherapy." *Journal of Counseling Psychology,* 19 (3), 259-261.

Laing, R. D.
 1960 *The Divided Self.* Chicago: Quadrangle Books.

Maier, H. W.
 1965 *Three Theories of Child Development.* New York: Harper and Row.

Pierce, R., and Schauble, P. G.
 1969 "Responsibility for Therapy: Counselor, Client or Who?" *The Counseling Psychologist,* 1:71-77.

Pietrofesa, J. J., and Vriend J.
 1971 *The Counselor as a Professional.* Itasca, Ill.: F. E. Peacock.

Stefflre, B.
 1970 "Counseling in the Total Society: A Primer." In W. Van Hoose, and J. J. Pietrofesa, *Counseling and Guidance in the Twentieth Century.* Boston: Houghton Mifflin, pp. 251-266.

Traxler, A.E.
 1970 "Guidance and Counseling—An Eclectic Point of View." In W. Van Hoose, and J. J. Pietrofesa, *Counseling and Guidance in the Twentieth Century.* Boston: Houghton Mifflin, pp. 281-295.

Chapter 5 Dealing with Ambiguity

INTRODUCTION The neophyte counselor soon learns that the stated initial reason for requesting an interview may only be a means of gaining entrance into the counselor's office. A poignant example was recently quoted by Ann Landers:

> *Dear Ann:* For years I've been meaning to write to you as a joke, to see if I could fool you into believing my letter was legitimate. Now I am writing the real thing. Two months ago my sister was killed in a car accident. Her boy friend, Mike, was driving and I was in the car, too. We weren't even scratched. The accident was not Mike's fault. Everyone knows that, but I can't help hating him just the same. My folks keep inviting Mike over because they feel sorry for him. They don't hold him responsible, but I'm getting so I can't stand the sight of the guy. I've tried to talk to my school counselor but I can't get the word out. I end up pre-

tending I came to talk about something else. Can you help me?

THE PRETENDER

Dear Pretender: Writing to me was a giant step in the right direction. Now you must unburden yourself to your school counselor. Take this column in as an Icobreaker. Hand it to the counselor and say, "This is my letter." The rest will come.

Not all clients have an Ann Landers (1969) on hand to intercede for them. Consequently, the counselor must be aware of the necessity to facilitate openness in the counselee. He/She must be effective in dealing with the real reason behind a client's appearance. This is especially true with students who request an interview ostensibly to discuss educational or vocational plans or to gain information about possible future courses of action. Therefore, it behooves the perceptive counselor to tolerate the uncertainty of not knowing exactly what the client really wishes to discuss until a relationship is established which will allow the process of counseling to continue. This capacity in the counselor can be defined as tolerance for ambiguity. Ambiguity itself has been defined as "the lack of structure or the presence of incompleteness or vagueness in a stimulus situation" (Patterson, 1966, p. 13). Blocher (1966) regards it further as "the degree of openness or uncertainty that exists in the minds of both counselor and client regarding what is supposed to happen next" (p. 161).

Specifically, a counselor can handle ambiguity if he/she does not think in either/or, or black/white terms, and is able to live without answers. He/She is also able to refrain from making judgments about the client and from asking specific questions which often serve only to provide the counselor with unnecessary factual information and take the focus off the client.

Bordin (1968) has written of "ambiguity . . . as an attribute of stimulus situations. Some stimulus situations do not elicit any single response or demand the same response from everybody . . . Ambiguity is that attribute of a stimulus situation whose demand character on different persons is different; that is, its demand character is variable" (pp. 149ff). He sees ambiguity as serving three functions in the therapeutic relationship (pp.158-159):

First, it capitalizes on the principle that people invest ambiguous stimuli with those responses that are most heavily laden with the unique aspects of their life history.
Second, ambiguity in therapeutic relationships becomes a medium for finding out important things about a personality similar to a projective situation.
Third, ambiguity helps to insure the effectiveness of the well-timed interpretation.

It would be a misconception to conclude that the above aspects are separate and distinct. They are, as Bordin (1968) notes, "Dynamically interrelated parts of an organic whole" (p. 151). Thus, it must be emphasized that the counselor not only must be able to tolerate ambiguity, but must accept his/her own responsibilities in the counseling relationship that can lead to an ambiguous situation for the client. The counselor is directly responsible for the presence and absence of topics that either are or are not discussed, the relationship that either does or does not develop so that the client feels he/she can discuss what is most important to him/her, and the making or not making of plans designed to aid the client to achieve his/her goals.

This is not to say that counseling is either an aimless procedure or a social conversation; it is quite the opposite. What we wish to emphasize is that in order for meaningful counseling to take place, a relationship must be established that will allow the client to feel "free," and will allow for release of any tensions so that mutual trust, confidence, and esteem can be established. It would seem, as a natural consequence then, that it would be of critical importance for the client to feel accepted and understood. The counselee must feel truly cared for by the counselor. Truax and Carkhuff (1967, pp. 39ff) have found, for example, that empathy must be accurate in order for counseling to be meaningful. Thus, the client must feel free to talk about his/her feelings openly and reveal perceptions and thoughts that he/she would not ordinarily expose to others.

It is quite apparent that this end will not be easy for the counselor to effect. Indeed, the counselor in a creative search for more effective ways to aid the client progress in self-development must work on a ". . capacity to tolerate internal conflict, his willingness to suspend judgment. He (must learn) not to be uncomfortable in the presence of unanswered questions or unresolved differences" (Gardner, 1965, p. 38).

The counselor must continue to work in this capacity to suspend judgment often in the face of contradictory statements and evidence until he/she can come to some decision as to how to proceed to help the client best. It cannot be emphasized too often that counselors are made, not born, and that ambiguity can have an effect on them also. Consequently, the counselor must work ceaselessly at his/her own growth. (See Appendix). As Rogers (1961) has put it:

> The degree to which I can create relationships which facilitate the growth of others as separate persons is a measure of the growth I have achieved in myself. In some respects this is a disturbing thought, but it is also a promising or challenging one. It would indicate that, if I am interested in creating helping relationships, I have a fascinating lifetime job ahead of me, stretching and developing my potentialities in the direction of growth. [p. 43]

This statement by Rogers suggests that being is a process, not an event; that being, if it implies a rather static, dormant state is not the condition in which any self-respecting counselor will, by choice, remain. On the contrary, we suggest the dynamic, evolving process of being and becoming is the proper personal status of the counselor.

Ambiguity and Counseling Structure Regardless of the amount of structure provided by the counselor, the counselee retains ambiguous and ambivalent feelings about the counseling relationship. Counselee ambiguity can provide a "growth vehicle" upon which the counselor can focus. The counselee can "project" his/her own feelings on this ambiguous relationship. The counselor then helps the client to become aware of his/her attitudes and feelings and to be better able to handle them in an effective manner.

On the other hand, Brammer and Shostrom (1960) caution:

> Too much ambiguity for some clients can allow them to become filled with anxiety in their attempts to make something secure and structured out of the relationship. For example, being too permissive with clients early in the counseling process and encouraging too free exploration of feelings may make them panicky . . . [p. 164]

Apparently, the counselor is most effective in handling this dimension if much of the initial structure provided is gradually faded from the counseling session, e.g., the counselor resorts to less questioning. Gradually, directions and guidelines provided by the counselor are reduced. Carlson and Mayer (1970) discuss this procedure with elementary school youth.

> Play objects are familiar to the child; therefore they are often used temporarily to help put him at ease and reduce the initial anxiety in the counseling session. In this situation, the play media initially becomes the stimulus for verbal interaction or other types of communication. The fading process applied to play media is one of making play prompts less and less available to the child. Through the gradual withdrawal of play objects (or counseling prompts), the child is given increasing amounts of responsibility for verbal participation in the counseling setting. For example, the counselor could choose gradually to eliminate specific play objects with increasing interviews. In this process, we help the child to become less and less dependent on the presence of 'physical crutches' for communication while maintaining a relatively low level of anxiety. [p. 4]

This is not to imply that the counselor provides purposely vague statements to the counselee. In fact, clear communication models should be used. However, some ambiguity is always involved when counseling is "counselee-centered" and not "counselor-centered." Counselor behavior is less ambiguous and perhaps most clear when the counselor directs and tells the counselee what to do.

Little ambiguity occurs during counseling when the counselor closes or narrows the counselee's options. Close-ended questions which can only result in "yes" and "no" answers eliminate most ambiguity. Open-ended questions (How did that happen?) or statements (Tell me more about it) allow for a wider range of counselee responses. Blocher (1966) writes:

> Techniques that move the interview along the dimension of ambiguity in either direction are not necessarily good or bad in themselves. Their value depends entirely on the results that are obtained. Many beginning counselors, however,

overwork techniques of the narrow 'yes' or 'no' type and are unable to use the more imaginative leads that increase ambiguity. Continued use of closed questions may seriously hamper communication. On the other hand, the use of completely uncontrolled ambiguity may be threatening to both counselor and client under some circumstances. [p. 161]

Initial Phases of the Interview In the initial phases of the interview, the client may be "testing" the counselor to see if threatening statements will be accepted. Once the client feels able to discuss his/her feelings openly, the counselor can help the client to begin to gain insight into the impact of these statements and help the client to place them in perspective. In order to illustrate this concept, let us consider the following interview as an example of how a counselor was able to aid a client to gain some self-insight as opposed to freely dispensing some information. The client was a twenty-two-year-old college student.

Counselor: Well, hello, Betty, what can I help you with?
Client: I'm interested in finding out about the field of Public Health.
Counselor: I see—you're considering this as a possible future career?
Client: Well, yes and no. I've heard about a grant that's offered and I think I might like to try for it.*
Counselor: The grant appeals to you even though you don't know much about the field—is that it?
Client: Yes, I am interested in science and wonder if this would be a means of getting on in the field.
Counselor: Tell me more about your interest in this, Betty.
Client Bacteriology is fascinating, and I like biology and, then too, I could use a . . . see, bacteriology and biochemistry are very closely related and I could take one or the other. So that . . . see, I work for the City Health Department now and I'm sure

---

*Note that throughout this initial phase there are opportunities wherein the counselor could refer the client to an occupational file or handbook, thus closing off the ambivalence clearly indicated by the client.

that when I get my degree and apply for entrance to graduate school there that they would bend over backwards to give me a good recommendation.

Counselor: You'd like to use this as a way of getting to graduate school.

Client: Yes, and since they're ... it would not be difficult, I think, to get a—this is the United States Department of Public Health or going into Public Health.

Counselor: Um hum.

Client: And I think since they need people it wouldn't be too difficult to get a grant. Well, at least it's something to think about definitely and it's within—it's possible; it's within reason. Other than that, when I get my degree I'll have to work a couple years before I can start graduate school.

Counselor: So this would help you save a couple of years.

Client: Well, yeah, there seems to be that there is a possibility—something I can look to. I haven't been able to figure out any other way of doing this. Maybe that's been my whole trouble, not being able to see how I was going to manage.

Counselor: You haven't been able to organize things yourself so you could accomplish what you wanted to; is that it?

Client: Like going to medical school. I haven't got a dime. Well this is, I think may have ... be discouraging and make me think well, that isn't what I want; because you get through school, and no money, and then you find you can't get a loan, and 'course that's not promising I ever will get through school. Anyway that's the story.*

---

* The relationship seems to have been established at this stage and the client feels able to confide in the counselor.

Counselor: All these tied in together really get you down.

Client: Yeah, I don't know I just . . . When I first started to school I didn't . . . I started to school I didn't want to go in the first place, but I went 'cause I thought if I didn't then I'll never get to go anywhere. The first two years I didn't care about grades—I was interested in learning, and so I made A's and B's—a few C's, but my grade average was very good. And then I started getting interested in the grades, and from that time on I haven't been able to do anything.

Counselor: The harder you tried, the worse you seemed to do . . .

Client: And I can't . . . I don't know why that should be, but I can't seem to . . . when the chips are down I can't work. I can't really work under pressure; I just give up. It's easier to give up or change your mind and start something else than to knuckle down and really work. So this morning, though, I had a basal metabolism test run, and in another month I'll have a protein iodine, and my doctor thinks that my thyroid is underactive and that makes me so tired. That may be a contributing . . . I hope that there's something physically wrong so that I . . . And I know part of the trouble must be that when I'm discouraged or lose interest in something it's much easier to do something else and say I'm tired than knuckle down and work.

Counselor: It's easier to sort of, ah, to go to sleep than to do?

Client: Well, I never a . . . I never really worried about the future. I always thought, well, I'll always be able to do something, even if it's just scrubbing floors. There's no real worry about having enough to eat or anything like that. So I say well, wait another year; maybe something else will turn up. But this has been going on too long, and this is very bad. I mean this is even worse than low grades, with an ability to make either rapid or steady progress. So I don't know.

Counselor: But now you sort of feel that . . . well, that you have to be thinking very seriously about the future and . . .

Client: Yes. I'm 22 now, and really the only thing . . . well, I could do office work or I could be a technician again, and that's all I'm equipped for, and I think of my classmates that I started out with, and many of them are getting their Master's degrees now, and here I am still flying around not knowing just what I want to do. And so this is not bad because you have, I guess, . . . if you're a late bloomer such as I was, that I didn't really grow up enough to take care of myself until I was about 21. But I mean, how long does it take to reach that state of maturity where you can really make decisions and stick by them. And I think it's about time that I reached that stage.

It is quickly apparent that the interview has progressed to the point where the client is concerned with not only, "What to do?" but also with, "Can I do it?" As Holland (1965) has noted, the answer to the latter question will often set the outer limits to the former (p. 214). So, often the danger that presents itself in an interview of this nature is that the counselor will either attempt to reassure the client ("Don't you think you may be worrying too much?") or cause the interview to progress according to the counselor's evaluation of the client's ability rather than the client's evaluation of *himself/herself.* There is often a considerable discrepancy. As Bordin (1968) has noted in this regard, "A directive lead seems to be a demand for a client to talk about a very specific topic in restricted terms as contrasted with a nondirective lead which is a more general invitation to communicate, sometimes including a relatively unrestricted designation of a topic" (p. 156).

The Self-Concept in Counseling The importance of the self-concept can be noted in the client's comments about herself. It is apparent that she has real questions about her ability "to do." Consequently, the counselor felt it necessary to deal with these concerns rather than attempting to direct the interview to a premature conclusion through introducing educational-vocational concepts that would not, in all probability, have any lasting value. It must be noted in this regard that giving the client information may often be a waste of time if he/she is either not ready to use it in making plans or in pursuing a particular course of action. Thus, the importance of the counselor's ability to tolerate the ambiguity of the counseling process is underlined. Too often, the counselor is prone to prematurely diagnose a situation and then to proceed on the basis of this diagnosis. The counselor, of course will, and must, make some analysis of the present difficulties of the client. However, there is considerable variance in the evidence that we have concerning the value of the counselor's initial diagnosis (Tyler, 1969, pp. 67-97). This is because the inferences the counselor makes will often turn out to be erroneous when other information is divulged by the client or more evidence is presented. Thus, it must be emphasized that any diagnosis made by the counselor must be regarded as tentative and subject to continual reevaluation. The counselor should be ready to suspend judgment and "stay with" the client until the situation has become as clear as possible to the counselor and the client is ready to proceed in a certain direction.

Later Stages of the Interview In the interview presented in this chapter, the counselor judged it necessary to help the client understand her own attitudes, values, and self-perceptions before more concrete courses of action or decisions could be considered. As Callis (1963) has stated, "Clients who seek assistance from counselors generally have either a present or perceived inadequacy in their behavior repertoire" (p. 179). These inadequacies are generally caused by either a lack of experience or distorted perceptions. Counseling, then, can be seen as one means of discovering these inadequacies and formulating ways of correcting them. However, it must be noted that in the eyes of the writers, the perception of these inadequacies must come as a result of client discovery before any lasting steps can be taken by the client to correct them. Consequently, it is often important for the counselor to help the client reduce his/her level of anxiety before he/she can proceed to the solving of what is, seemingly, an immediate problem. This can be illustrated by another excerpt from the interview discussed previously.

Following is a continuation of the first interview with this particular client.

Client: I think I want to study something with biology—either that or bacteriology ... I keep coming back to it and think about it, and then the more I think about it the more it sounds like it would be one field that I could really stick to, and then — this probably would be the most sensible thing to do because I'd like that kind of work, and then there's the possibility that I could go on to medical school, and this is one lure it has. Then the alternative is if I didn't go into medical school I'd still be in a field which held a lot of interest.

Counselor: It would also give you some protection.

Client: Yeah, something to fall back on, as the old saying goes. So now what I have to do is find my inspiration. I think that maybe I'm just exhausted because I don't know. . . .

Counselor: If only you could get some sense of direction.

Client: Yeah. I haven't been able to study since about March. I just dragged all day; drag home and drag to school, I don't know. The thing that bothers me is that other people do so much more and work so much harder and I just can't seem to do it. And I require eight, nine, ten hours sleep. Any less than that I just drag all day long. I think this is not . . . then I like to try to limit my sleep to seven or eight hours a night, because you can't work and go to school and then sleep for ten hours a night. There isn't time.

Counselor: You even wonder sometimes whether there's something wrong with you.

Client: Yeah. And my girl friend—five hours and she's wide awake and ready to go. If I had five hours of sleep, I think one week and I'd fall over, and this may be that my thyroid is overactive and this could possibly be part of the trouble. But I've always been a long sleeper. And I'm slow moving. I walk slowly, and I'm just sluggish all the way around. And I noticed that recently people say, "Well, it's your imagination" but I'm not as sharp as I used to be. When I got out of high school and I first started college I could learn something much easier ... much more easily, and more quickly than I do now. Now when I learn something it takes effort, and I don't know why this should be. I think, I don't see why your mental capacity should decrease; I just can't reason that they do. And that may be because I let myself get run down. That could be a part.

Counselor: You don't like this about yourself very much.

Client: No, I don't. I don't like to think that gee, maybe by the time I'm fifty I'll be a complete idiot. No, not really, but it does. I have noticed it. People say, "Well, that's your imagination. You're studying harder things now," but that's not so. Even in the easy courses that before would have been a breeze, they're a drag, and I have to make myself work at them, where before it was just ... I think it was because I was interested in learning. And the enthusiasm just made it easy. Because what I'm interested in is easy for me. Not just because I like to work; if I'm not interested in it then it's not so easy. But now it's just that everything is like that.

Counselor: So no matter how you try to explain it, you always come back to you?

Client: Um hum. I used think I was punishing myself and these things. I don't know why I just can't knuckle down and study. 'Cause nothing I've studied so far has been so difficult that I couldn't learn it, and yet I've let myself fail courses, and I've got C's, and I've missed A's where I should have easily made A's, just because I won't study the way I should.

Counselor: So you're thinking sometimes, maybe, why am I doing this to myself?

Client: Um hum. I used to think I was punishing myself and that's silly. But maybe I am. Maybe I don't have the self-respect that I should have and so I'm forever torturing myself by doing things ... I keep doing things that will prevent me from realizing my ambitions. This is a theory that I have about myself, but I don't know enough to ... why should I punish myself? Maybe I am. Someone used to tell me all the time, she'd say well, what am I trying to prove? And I was always puzzled, and well I didn't think I was trying to prove anything. And she said, well, I was just trying to show ... that I was just trying to do ... show that I was as good as any man, and by ... showing this by doing a man's job and studying something like medicine which is predominantly held by men in the medical profession. That's what she thinks, and she may be right, I don't know that either.

Counselor: You don't think that it's true though?

Client: Well, it could be true in part. See I have four older brothers, and I resented them as I was growing up; I resented their freedom and they got to go places I never got to go and did things, and then I'd ask well why couldn't I do those things, and my mother would say, "Well, girls just don't do that," and I think in part that may have been it. So I'm left now to realize these things. At least I can understand what my mother was doing and I have no more resentment, so why should I now be trying to prove something? I'm just as good as they are. So I don't know. But at the place I worked they wanted me to study math, and they were doing all they could to encourage me to stay with the company. The last pay raise I got was a double increment. Then I kept thinking, here are these draftsmen who haven't had any college training and they make more than I do, and that made me feel very uncomfortable. And I thought, gee, if I had a Master's degree in mathematics and I was in charge of the entire computer programming, I still couldn't make as much money as an engineer, and this bothered me, so I left Edison and went back to school. So that may be that I still have resentments against men, and maybe I am trying to prove that I'm just as good as any man. And that may in some way ... that's what bothers me; I think well maybe I'm just trying to prove that fact and that I really don't want to be a doctor, but that's just the one way I can prove it to myself and other people. But then I turn around on the other side and I've always dreamed about nothing else. Even when I was a small child I wanted to become a doctor and I used to play at it and dream about it—and that's on the other side.

Counselor: You're not sure which of these is the reason behind your ...?

Client: I don't know which one it's ... I don't know really why I want to become a doctor. I've tried to think well when I'm asked this question—I surely will be asked it when I apply for admission to the medical school—what will I say? Why do I want to be a doctor? And I don't have a very good answer for it, except that's what I've always wanted to do—I've always wanted to be able to help people, and people say to me, "Well, there are other ways to help people," but this is something I've always wanted to do. And I think this field of Public Health would be something I should try to make up my mind for, because there are many avenues of ... you could branch out into this or that. You could study viruses or you could study biochemistry or maybe go to medical school such as I think I'd like to do. I think that is one . . . maybe something concrete that I can start working on.

It may be seen that, in the latter stages of the first interview, the client is beginning to move towards a more positive perception of herself as well as becoming ready to make some concrete plans concerning her future. There is still a considerable amount of ambivalence in her statements but she seems to be moving from doubting whether she *can* do something concrete to a belief that she is able to achieve a realistic goal.

The client was seen for five more interviews, at the end of which she seemed to have come to a point of resolving her conflicts to the extent that she was able to cope with them.

The preceding is presented as an example of what Tyler (1960, pp. 475-477) has termed "minimum change therapy" wherein the object of counseling is seen as not a major reorganization of personality but a minimum change in psychological direction.

The tolerance for ambiguity discussed earlier seems to have been manifested by the counselor in this particular instance. He was able to continue to communicate with the client on her own terms without "pushing" the interview.

Importance of Tolerance for Ambiguity in Counseling It may be noted herein that this capacity or personality characteristic of counselors to tolerate ambiguity has been found by Brams (1961) to be the principal variable of counselor behavior related to effectiveness in the counseling interview (p. 30). Gruberg (1969), moreover, in a study involving in-service counselors, concluded that there was a significant relationship between tolerance of ambiguity and counseling orientation (pp. 119-124). He found, further, that tolerance of ambiguity was also related to the amount of talking a counselor did in the interview situation. Counselors with a high tolerance of ambiguity spent significantly less time speaking in the interview than counselors with a low tolerance. There is, as well, evidence that indicates that the greater the amount of counselor talk in the interview, the greater the amount of rigidity in structure.

What happens is that the counselor attempts to control the ambiguity in the counseling interview through attempting to overly structure the situation. The counselor will then limit the content of the interview either through questioning the client on certain specific aspects or by stating what areas or topics may be expected to be discussed. For example:

"Well, we're here to talk about college. ."
"I'm sorry, but I'm not a psychologist. . . ."
"I think that's something you'll have to solve by yourself. . . ."
"I thought you came here to talk about jobs. . . ."
"What I'm interested in is. . . ."
"You said your husband. . . ."

There is also evidence that a significant relationship exists between tolerance of ambiguity and the effectiveness of counselor responses. This, in all probability, is due to the fact that the counselor who weighs the import of client statements before making a response will respond more accurately. This indicates that the *pace* of the interview must be a leisurely one if communication is to be as effective as possible. And, indices of communication have been found to be "the best predictors of level of functioning in the helping role" (Carkhuff, 1969, p. 271). The emphasis that this would lead us to in counseling is that characterized by Daane and McGreevy (1966) as used by the "dynamic" counselor with an intrapersonal focus (p. 267). This focus gives less emphasis to normative assessments and "increased concern for an experiencing of affect. Self-awareness is obtained through exploring the client's own feelings." It has been shown to be effective by both Kinnick and Shannon (1965) and Dolan (1964). However, this approach is not congruent with either a "behavioral" (Krumboltz, 1964) model of counseling or what has been termed a "milieu" (Daane and McGreevy, 1966) model. In both of these approaches, emphasis is placed on specific cultural values and past client behavior. Change may be seen in the "dynamic" model to come from *within*. And, this is a major responsibility of the *counselor*. For, "There is substantial basis for believing that to be effective, counselors and therapists must be shaped by what is effective for the client. Facilitative agents do not operate in a vacuum. While in process, they must be able to trust their motives; ultimately, they must be able to trust the feedback they get from their clients, and this feedback must indicate that on the relevant indices the client has improved" (Berenson and Carkhuff, 1967, p. 440).

SUMMARY

It is the position of the writers that, in order for a change in behavior to take place, the counselor must be able to aid the client to work through ambivalent attitudes and feelings regarding particular situations before effective action can be taken. In short, the counselor must be able to tolerate ambiguity, i.e., be able to deal effectively with a lack of structure or the presence of vagueness or incompleteness in the counseling endeavor. This ability in the counselor helps to establish the necessary ingredients of a helping relationship, e.g., acceptance, freedom, empathy, and understanding. During the initial phases of the interview, the aforementioned counselor can allow the client to discuss his/her feelings and give direction in contrast to the counselor who necessarily seeks closure. Further, one who is tolerant of vagueness will not lapse into premature diagnosis.

It must be emphasized in this regard that a major point for the counselor to be aware of is ambivalence. Conflicting feelings on the part of the client toward any situation, any person, should immediately become a focus of attention on the part of the counselor. Still, the counselor should be prepared to "stay with" the client and remain tentative in any conclusions while the client works through the resolution of the ambivalence.

Finally, there is substantial basis for feeling that tolerance of ambiguity is an effective dimension of any human encounter. To paraphrase Berenson and Carkhuff (1967, p. 439ff), there are a certain number of human encounters and facilitative techniques which are not entities in themselves. Some ways and means of facilitating these conditions may be more effective than others in encouraging personal growth on the part of the client. It is incumbent on the part of the counselor to incorporate into his/her reactions a tolerance for the ambiguity of the client so as to aid him/her to understand his/her past behavior and to make more effective plans for the future.

REFERENCES

Berenson, Bernard G., and Carkhuff, Robert R.
   1967 *Sources of Gain in Counseling and Psychotherapy.* New York: Holt, Rinehart and Winston.

Blocher, Donald H.
   1966 *Developmental Counseling* New York. The Ronald Press. Copyright © 1900, The Ronald Press Company, New York.

Bordin, Edward S.
1968 *Psychological Counseling*, 2nd ed. New York: Appleton-Century-Crofts, Educational Division, Meredith Corporation.

Brammer, L. M., and Shostrom, E. L.
1960 *Therapeutic Psychology*. Englewood Cliffs, N.J.: Prentice-Hall.

Brams, Jerome M.
1961 "Counselor Characteristics and Effective Communication in Counseling." *Journal of Counseling Psychology*, 8.25-30.

Callis, Robert.
1963 "Counseling." *Review of Educational Research*, 33:179-187.

Carkhuff, Robert.
1969 "The Prediction of the Effects of Teacher-Counselor Education: The Development of Communication and Discrimination Selection Indexes." *Counselor Education and Supervision*, 8:265-272.

Carlson, J., and Mayer, G. Roy
1970 "Fading: A Behavioral Procedure to Increase Independent Behavior." Mimeographed. Detroit: Wayne State University. Also in *The School Counselor*, published by American Personnel and Guidance Association, Washington, D.C.

Daane, Calvin, and McGreevy, C. Patrick.
1966 "The Counseling Process and Function." *Review of Educational Research*, 36:264-273.

Dolan, G. Keith.
1964 "Effects of Individual Counseling." *Personnel and Guidance Journal*, 42:914-919. Reprinted with permission of the publisher, American Personnel and Guidance Association, Washington, D.C.

Gardner, John.
1965 *Self-Renewal*. New York: Harper and Row.

Gruberg, Ronald.
1969 "A Significant Counselor Personality Characteristic: Tolerance of Ambiguity." *Counselor Education and Supervision*, 8:119-124.

Holland, Glen.
1965 *Fundamentals of Psychotherapy*. New York: Holt, Rinehart and Winston.

Kinnick, Bernard, and Shannon, Jack.
1965 "The Effect of Counseling on Peer Group Acceptance of Socially Rejected Students." *The School Counselor*, 12:162-166. Reprinted with permission of the publisher, American Personnel and Guidance Association, Washington, D.C.

Krumboltz, John.
1964 "Parable of the Good Counselor." *Personnel and Guidance Journal*, 43:118-126. Reprinted with permission of the publisher, American Personnel and Guidance Association, Washington, D.C.

Landers, Ann.
1969 "Help Me Handle Hate for Mike." *Detroit Free Press*, March 23. By

permission of Ann Landers, *Detroit Free Press*, and Publishers-Hall Syndicate.

Patterson, C. H.
    1966 *Theories of Counseling and Psychotherapy*. New York: Harper and Row.

Rogers, Carl R.
    1961 *On Becoming a Person*. Boston: Houghton Mifflin.

Truax, Charles, and Carkhuff, Robert.
    1967 *Toward Effective Counseling and Psychotherapy: Theories and Practice*. Chicago: Aldine.

Tyler, Leona E.
    1960 "Minimum Change Therapy." *Personnel and Guidance Journal,* 38:475-479. Reprinted with permission of the publisher, American Personnel and Guidance Association, Washington, D.C.
    1969 *The Work of the Counselor*. 3rd ed. New York: Appleton-Century-Crofts, Educational Division, Meredith Corporation.

Chapter 6 Authentic Behavior in the Counseling Relationship

INTRODUCTION Authenticity has over the years been considered a basic ingredient of the helping relationship. It has been felt that if the counselor did not provide a sufficient degree of authenticity, change could not occur within the client. We basically agreed with this position in 1971 and still do. Yet, the concept of authenticity presents a dilemma for those of us engaged in counseling or in counselor education. We recognize that authentic behavior by the healthy counselor facilitates positive growth in the client. On the other hand, the last thing we want from an unhealthy counselor is authentic behavior, for in this case such behavior can be quite destructive. Furthermore, the concept of authenticity has allowed some "counselors" to say that "training is unnecessary. All I need to do is be myself." That is a basic misrepresentation of the entire notion of authentic being. An article written in 1976 reflects some of the concern many have felt. First, it calls attention to the proliferation of gimmickry in the field. Second, it raises the question of what to do with someone reflecting basically unhealthy motives in the counseling endeavor, i.e., greed. Dr. Verstunk is "authentic" and also destructive.

Celebrity Interview

Other professional journals have instituted as regular features interviews with noted giants in the field.[1] Believing that such a practice is noteworthy, we pondered for several moments in order to select an eminent authority. We finally decided to interview Dr. Hans Verstunck, the founder of Verstunck Therapy. Dr. Verstunck's history is indeed interesting. He was toilet trained by three weeks, and consequently nicknamed Hans "Anal" Verstunck. Dr. Verstunck is basically eclectic. In fact his motto, "We steal from everyone," was borne out when he was indicted by the grand jury on three counts of grand larceny and by the federal government for income tax evasion.

Interviewer: Dr. Verstunck, this is indeed a great pleasure for me.

Dr. Verstunck: Yes it is. But before we get started, I'd prefer we be informal. I'm a human being just like you. I zip my pants up every morning. Please call me by my first name—Dr. or Sir.

Interviewer: Could you please provide the research and philosophical underpinnings for Verstunck Therapy?

Dr. Verstunck: Certainly. Our earliest research in the Verstunck Lab demonstrated inconclusively that the human being has an aura which we labeled immediately the "Verstuncken." The "Verstuncken" is a reflection of body defenses which we call the "Verduncken." The "Verstuncken" and the "Verduncken" come from childhood impulses named "Verfuncken." In our therapy we inflate the "Verfuncken" by reducing the "Verduncken" and changing the overall "Verstuncken." And if you believe this, I've got some swampland up north I'll let you have cheap.

[1] Reprinted with permission from John J. Pietrofesa, Robert Clifton, and Barry Markman. Celebrity Interview." *Michigan Personnel and Guidance Journal,* 1976, 7(2), 3-8.

Interviewer: Yes, all right Dr. Verstunck. Could you tell us about your famous therapeutical approaches.

Dr. Verstunck: That can be difficult. After all we do service 78,000 patients. But . . .

Interviewer: Wow! Excuse me. Seventy-eight thousand patients—that's quite a few. How do you ever do that?

Dr. Verstunck: Groups.

Interviewer: That is still quite a few groups. How many actual groups do you have?

Dr. Verstunck: Two.

Interviewer: Two! That's thirty-nine thousand people in a group!

Dr. Verstunck: Yes. I used to do individual therapy, but at $30 an hour it was quite taxing. My new approach means I only work two hours a week and make $121,680,000 a year. Our clinic was second to General Motors last year in profits after taxes. Of course we did not pay any taxes because we are a nonprofit, altruistic organization. We did have difficulty finding a place to hold our groups but now that the Detroit Lions have moved to Pontiac, we use Tiger Stadium.

Interviewer: Isn't it difficult to do therapy in such large groups?

Dr. Verstunck: No, I use a co-leader. You'll see him up in the stands selling popcorn and peanuts between interventions. The more popcorn you buy, the less confrontative he is. It is good popcorn—right from Verstunck farms. After the marathon he sells Verstunck T-shirts emblazoned with the Verstunck philosophy "Nobody likes a sickie."

Interviewer: Tell us some specific techniques.

Dr. Verstunck: We make good use of bats.

Interviewer: Bataca bats! Terrific! I hear patients work off their hostilities and anxieties by hitting the floor and even each other with these bats.

Dr. Verstunck: No! Baseball bats! We hit patients in the head when they get hostile or don't pay their bills. We also do nude group work.

Interviewer: The patients must really enjoy that.

Dr. Verstunck: No. It is only for the therapists. We take off our clothes and reduce our Verstunckens! That's another thing we are really into—sex therapy.

Interviewer: How did you prepare yourself to be effective in so difficult an area?

Dr. Verstunck: Pornography flicks. I visited every movie house in a three-hundred-mile area. Hours on end I sat and watched films. I want to make a point with your readers. The human body is beautiful. There is nothing obscene about it. And another thing, people should not be ashamed of visiting a movie house to see humans engaged in the sex act. They should keep their heads high and not be fearful of narrow-minded and bigoted people.

Interviewer: Well said! Do you have any further advice?

Dr. Verstunck: Make sure they buy a loose fitting ski mask; it is difficult to breathe when the mask is tight. Oh yeah, also the mouth hole should be large enough for popcorn and . . .

Interviewer: Do you make much use of behavior modification?

Dr. Verstunck: Yes! If the group applauds my techiques the Goodyear Blintze swoops down over the stadium and drops three tons of M & M Candies evenly over the crowd. If they don't applaud, I flip a switch and all the toilets back up at once.

Interviewer: All right, all right. Dr. Verstunck, there are various conflicting interpretations of your therapy making the rounds. Can you give our readers the true essence of Verstunck philosophy?

Dr. Verstunck: Both readers or only one? Oh well! The essence is simple. Pure, unadultered, unmitigating hostility toward the patient.

Interviewer: Hostility? That is a different approach. How can being hostile possibly help the patient?

Dr. Verstunck: It teaches him he has no friends, including the therapist, thereby freeing the patient to help himself. Lord knows I'm not going to! I got problems of my own. My car needs a new muffler, I haven't washed my hair in weeks, and I got a piece of gum stuck to the roof of my mouth. See if you can get it out. Reach back here . . .

Interviewer: Never mind doctor. I'm sure you know Rogers talked about empathy and Jourard about authenticity as basic conditions of therapy. What are some conditions basic to your approach?

Dr. Verstunck: Unconditional negative distaste. I offer all my patients, rich and poor, the same amounts of contempt.

Interviewer: I think I see. Are there any other schools of therapy which you consider antagonistic to your ideas?

Dr. Verstunck: Monte Hall's greedism—it teaches that money brings happiness. In fact, the truth is giving away money is the true source of happiness. That's why my fee goes up each year. Say, how would you like to be a little happier?

Interviewer: I'm confused.

Dr. Verstunck: Your Verdunck is out of whack. How about one of my bicentennial Verstunck treatments? Only 1776 dollars—American. I can get you a good seat—section 15, row G, seat 12. You can't see home plate, but that is o.k. because I lead the group from second base.

Interviewer: Are your therapeutic endeavors successful?

Dr. Verstunck: What a ridiculous question! Of course. Some patients have been with us for over twenty years.

Interviewer: Other experts in therapy suggest that success and goal accomplishment are achieved only after the patient has left therapy and is able to function without the therapist.

Dr. Verstunck: Success for the patient maybe, but how about the poor therapist. Obviously that bullshitten was written by a college professor who doesn't know what it is like in the "real" world. I have to make a living. Look at it this way—what would I do for a living if everyone was healthy? The goal of therapy is self-awareness—a never-ending process. I believe everyone needs my therapy! Let's see, 200,000,000 multiplied by $30—how much is that a week?

Interviewer: Dr. Verstunck, who would you say was the greatest influence in the development of your therapy techiniques?

Dr. Verstunck: I would have to say my father.

Interviewer: Was he an analyst too?

Dr. Verstunck: No, he was a chicken flicker.

Interviewer: And how did he influence your ideas?

Dr. Verstunck: When I was a boy of eight he put me on top of the porch and told me to jump into his arms. I expressed great fear, but he convinced me to jump. As I jumped he moved to the side so I could not reach him—I broke both of my legs. I still remember his words—told to me as I lay on the ground in pain—"Don't trust anybody, not even your father."

Interviewer: That seems like an awfully cruel thing to do to an eight-year-old boy.

Dr. Verstunck: Cruel! No! That was one of the nice things—most of the time he was mean to me.

Interviewer: It seems as if you had a difficult childhood Have you ever undergone therapy yourself?

Dr. Verstunck: What? Pay some weirdo $50 an hour so he could tell me how I hate my father. I don't hate my father—I despise my father. I used to hope that he would be pecked by a rabid chicken.

Interviewer: To change the subject slightly, how and where did you get your degree?

Dr. Verstunck: One day I was lighting my pipe and I noticed a large blot of ink on the matchbook cover. Under the ink it said, "If you can interpret this ink blot you may have what it takes to be an analyst." So I sent in my analysis to the Famous Analysts School and eight weeks later I had my degree.

Interviewer: Eight weeks—that doesn't appear to be a lot of training.

Dr. Verstunck: Maybe not for most people—but I'm a natural. Is the green man still on my shoulder?

Interviewer: I don't see any green man.

Dr. Verstunck: You obviously have a problem. One last exciting thing I want to mention is our own training programs. We are convinced that traditional programs which train psychologists and counselors are totally inadequate. We offer an alternative—a three-year educational Verstunck seminar. At the end of the first year each enrollee gets a certificate of merit and the title of Verstincker. At the conclusion of the second phase the students become full Verstunckers.

Interviewer: What does this allow the practitioner to do?

Dr. Verstunck: It allows him to Verstick it to the public.

Interviewer: Have you conducted any substantive, hard core research on the efficacy of your approaches, e.g., on the use of bats or large group work?

Dr. Verstunck: All of my research is hard core. In fact, so hard core I have three eminent citations from the President's Commission on Pornography. Well, I have to go now. We have a group about to start. We're going to try a new technique today. It is called, "Greenback, Greenback, who's got the greenback?"

Interviewer: Have you any final words of wisdom for our readers

Dr. Verstunck: I think it is only fitting that we close with the Verstunck Psalm. It is most meaningful.

The Verstunck Psalm

Verstunck is my shepherd,
He shall not want.
He riddeth me of green money.
He reduceth my income.
Yea, though he walketh through the valleys of my psyche,
I shall experience no growth.
My cup leaketh,
I anointeth his palm with lucre.
Only confrontation and exploitation follow me all the days of my life.
And I shall dwell in the House of Verstunck for years to come.

Interviewer: Don't you think that is in very bad taste?
Dr. Verstunck: Thank you. Of course. It is consistent with my therapy.

We would like to review the concept of the positive nature of authentic being, much as we did in the first edition, but then elaborate upon some of the negative elements, which were only touched upon earlier.

THE NEED FOR AUTHENTIC BEHAVIOR The American culture does not encourage authentic behavior. We are taught almost from conception to suppress, repress, or distort our behavior. As a result, we come to view much of ourselves as objectionable—something to be hidden from others. Anxiety develops—a fear of being found out, coupled with anger at the fact that we can't express what we feel. The tensions and anxieties that develop foster an unhealthy being. Certainly this contributes to the burgeoning pressures of human existence. Mental health statistics continue to reflect the extent of discontent and alienation in people. Coleman (1974) notes that 10,000,000 or more Americans are neurotic; 2,000,000 or more suffer from psychoses; 200,000 or more have attempted suicide; 4,000,000 or more have antisocial personalities; 1,500,000 juveniles and adults have been arrested for serious crimes; 500,000 are in penal institutions; 9,000,000 are labeled as alcoholics; 1,000,000 or more are dependent on hard drugs; and finally, there are 5,500,000 emotionally disturbed children and teenagers (p.10). Interestingly, Coleman points out that the resident population of state and county mental hospitals has declined and the first factor accountable is the "introduction of major tranquilizing and antidepressant drugs" (p. 19). While we might applaud the decline of the hospital population, a major reason for it is the introduction of a variety of drugs which are basically "behavior suppressants."

Kazan (1967) suggested in his novel, *The Arrangement*, that if one becomes too authentic, he or she might well be committed to an institution (pp.419-420). Furthermore, the absence of authenticity, by parents plays a role in the development of psychological distress in children. Much of this is based in the ambivalence of feelings displayed. The communication of the parents serves as a "disconfirmation" of the young person. Laing and Esterson (1964) write that the child's "authenticity has been subject to subtle, but persistent, mutilation, often quite unwillingly" (p. 91). Buber (1957) felt it important that a person's authenticity be confirmed. Yet, research suggests that this does not occur for those who become ill. For example, family members of the schizophrenic display behavior at variance with what they are saying (Haley, 1960). Singer (1961) substantiated the "disqualifying communication pattern" in schizophrenic families. Mark (1953) found mothers of schizophrenic children display attitudes of both excessive warmth and objective aloofness (pp. 485-489). Eisenberg and Kanner (1956) conclude that the typical autistic family does not provide warmth, or a growth-inducing atmosphere. Truax and Carkhuff (1967) summarized: "the parent's inauthenticity and lack of genuineness were suggested by their frequent references to 'observing' their children, as though they were clinical subjects" (p. 119). Such "clinical" observation strips the interaction of any being in the moment between the parent and child. Schizophrenics not only see others treating them in this fashion, they also see themselves in this fashion.

> People weren't real and in fact neither was I. I could step back and actually watch myself performing in a play or a movie. Yes, that's it exactly. I was an actor performing on a stage and I was sitting there watching me say lines that I had been taught, but that I really did not feel or mean. I was kind where I did not want to be. I was being the phony that all through my life others had taught me to be. It wasn't real. It was a dream, I wasn't real.

This lack of authenticity not only affects the schizophrenic or psychotic but also the "normal" person. Jourard (1964) wrote, "I believe, and I am not alone in this belief, that man is sick—not just neurotic and psychotic people; but so-called 'normal' man, too—because he hides his real self in his transactions with others" (p. 60). The lack of authenticity, then, pervades everyday life. Jourard and Whitman (1971) continue:

> Much of human life is best described as impersonation. We are role players, everyone of us. We say that we feel things we do not feel. We say that we did things we did not do. We pretend that we are loving when we are full of hostility. We pretend that we are calm and indifferent when we are actually trembling with anxiety and fear. [p. 83]

NATURE OF AUTHENTIC BEHAVIOR

Definitions Various terms in the counseling literature are used synonymously with authenticity. Others are quite close in meaning. Authentic behavior is genuine or real—a being in touch with one's self. The authentic or genuine person is "freely and deeply" him/herself. Facades are discarded and role prescribed behavior is freeing rather than inhibiting or limiting. The authentic counselor implements him/herself during the counseling session. The authentic person is open to experience and existence. Cottingham (1966) wrote that the objective of authentic behavior "is to bring greater accord between the giveness of man's nature and the being of the world itself" (p. 329). Hansen et al. (1977) state, "Genuineness means that the counselor is able to be himself in the relationship. He does not wear a facade, and he is able to let his feelings operate in counseling as they are appropriate" (p. 136). Basically, then, genuineness is "being aware of one's values and beliefs, and when one acts, to always act consistently, never inconsistently, with those beliefs, values, and attitudes" (Eisenberg and Delaney, 1977, p. 40). Congruence, for the purpose of this book, can also be used interchangeably with genuineness and authenticity. The congruent therapist is a transparent therapist (Truax and Carkhuff, 1965, p. 4). Self-awareness on the part of the counselor enables the presentation of a real person to the client (Truax, 1963, p. 259). Several indicators reflect authenticity. Openness indicates a great degree of self-communication. The open person is aware of his or her own feelings, desires, beliefs, and dreams. Self-disclosure, the ability to reveal something significant about oneself to another person, is also an indicator of authenticity. Finally, spontaneity—that which proceeds without restraint and is freely reflective of the self—also is found within the authentic being. Egan (1975) feels that the effective helper "while being tactful (as part of his respect for others), is not constantly weighing what he says. He does not put a number of filters between his inner life and what he expresses to others" (p. 92).

Recent Research on Authenticity in Counseling Various studies prior to 1971 suggested the importance of authenticity in counseling. We will cite several of these studies briefly and then review more thoroughly the studies of the past six years. Halikides (1958) found that genuineness of the counselor was associated with case outcome at the .001 level of significance. In 1962, Rogers observed that the most successful therapists in dealing with the unmotivated, poorly educated, resistant, chronically hospitalized persons, were those who were real, reacted in a genuine way as persons, and who exhibited this genuineness in relationships with others. Gendlin and Geist (1962) reported that extremely low levels of genuineness tend to minimize the effects of higher levels of empathy and respect. Truax (1963) found that there was a significant tendency for therapists in improved cases to be rated higher in self-congruence during therapeutic sessions than therapists in non-improved or failure cases (p. 259). Demos (1964) found that the most successful counselors received better ratings on congruence and comfort than did the least successful counselors. A significant relationship has been found from moment to moment throughout therapy between transparency or self-congruence of the therapists and transparency or self-disclosure for the patient (Truax and Carkhuff, 1965, p. 8). Staudenmeier (1967) reported that one of the three most effective behavior classifications for less experienced counselors was the communication of "honesty'. Additionally, male counselees felt that the counselor's behavior was most ineffective when honesty was not communicated (p. 116). Shapiro et al. (1969) found that subjects disclosed themselves more deeply to persons offering the highest levels of genuineness, empathy, and warmth. This led to a more open, full relationship in and out of psychotherapy. Hountras and

Anderson (1969) supported this finding, i.e., there is a significant relationship between the three aforementioned relationship dimensions and self-exploration in all problem categories for clients (pp. 45-48). Truax et al. (1971) found that therapeutic gain with hospitalized patients was significantly greater on twenty-five personality measures for therapists offering high levels of empathy, genuineness, and respect, than for therapists offering low levels of those three dimensions.

High-level conditions of genuineness in counseling appear to encourage change outside the counseling situation. Zigon and Cannon (1974) found that group members whose leaders provided high levels of genuineness and respect transferred learnings outside of the group significantly more so than did their counterparts.

Culberson (1975) studied the effects of low-level functioning counselors on high and low-level functioning clients. The former groups were measured on criteria of genuineness, empathy, respect, and concreteness, while the latter groups were identified on criteria of involvement, spontaneity, and nondefensiveness. Counselors reflecting low levels of facilitative skills were ineffective. Most interesting was the finding that with low-level clients, the low-functioning counselors actually had negative effects upon their clients. Fischer et al. (1975), dividing clinical practitioners into psychodynamic, behavioristic, and humanistic orientations, found no significant difference among therapists of different orientation on a measure of genuineness. Altmann (1973) reported that "stayers" in counseling were provided higher levels of genuineness than did "leavers." Hayden (1975), investigating the relationship between verbal behavior and effectiveness of experienced therapists, found that the more effective the experienced therapist, the higher were the counselor levels of genuineness, positive regard, and empathy.

The research continues to suggest that authenticity or genuineness facilitates positive change in clients. Our two concluding quotes in 1971 still appear to be valid. Truax and Carkhuff (1967) stated, "These findings might mean that we should aim at being what we are in our human encounters—that we would openly be the feelings and attitudes that we are experiencing" (p. 142). The Combs et al. (1969) summarization is excellent.

> That is to say, the crucial question is not 'what' method, but the 'fit' of the method, its appropriateness to the self of the helper, to his purposes, his subjects, the situation.... We

now believe the important distinction between the good and poor helper with respect to methods is not a matter of his perception of methods per se, but the authenticity of whatever methods ho uses. There is already some evidence for this in our findings that good helpers are self-revealing, involved and identified. [pp. 75-76]

Self-Disclosure and Openness in Counseling One dimension intricately interwoven into the fabric of authenticity is psychological openness—an openness to new experience as contrasted to psychological closedness. Openness permits the person to "most effectively use the total self for adaptive purposes" (Allen and Whitely, 1968, p. 6). The psychologically closed person is a rigid person who reflects a great deal of dogmatism in his/her view of the world. Such a person is controlled and inhibited (Maslow, 1959). Mezzano (1969) stated:

> The person who is less dogmatic tends to be more aware of his own reactions to stimuli, less need to distort meanings and considers ideas mainly on their merits. Further, he experiences less threat and anxiety, and is more permissive... The more dogmatic individual is less aware of his reactions to stimuli, tends to distort meaning in relation to early beliefs, and is less permissive. [p. 64]

One might well view the closed-open system as a continuum with all individuals falling somewhere between the two extremes. On the one end of the continuum you have the person who is closed, repressed, insensitive, rigid, defensive, anxious, and unaware. On the other end of the continuum you have the open, expressive, secure, sensitive, permissive, flexible, and aware person.

Various studies have pointed to the importance of openness in counseling and have associated it with certain personality variables. Lee and Ehrlich (1971) found that close-minded persons held more negative beliefs about self and others, held more contradictory self-beliefs, engaged in more self-proselytizing, sought more status and power, reported more self-righteousness, and had a greater sense of martyrdom than did their open-minded counterparts. Cutler (1958) noted that generally the therapist's handling of conflict material (conflict for the therapist) was less adequate than the handling of material which was free of conflict. Allen (1967), investigating the relationship between counseling effectiveness and psychological openness, found that open counselors responded more to the feelings of clients than those who were less open. Furthermore, there was a direct relationship between supervisor ratings of effectiveness and counselor expression.

Johnson and Noonan (1972), studying acceptance and reciprocation of self-disclosure as related to the formation of trust, obtained results suggesting that trust increases when a person's self-disclosure is met with acceptance rather than rejection, and particularly when self-disclosure is reciprocated. Spiritas and Holmes (1971) found that interviewees revealed more to a "revealing" model than they did to a "non-revealing" model. Perceptions of counselor self-disclosure, mental health, and helpfulness are all positively correlated (May and Thompson, 1973). Furthermore, self-revealing therapists are judged more friendly, disclosing, trusting, intimate, helpful, and facilitating but also as less relaxed, strong, stable, and sensitive (Dies, 1973).

Self-disclosure begets self-disclosure (Jourard and Jaffe, 1970), but too much can be ineffective. Giannandrea and Murphy (1973) noted that an intermediate number of interviewer self-disclosures results in significantly more clients returning for a second contact than did few or many self-disclosures. Moderate self-disclosure increases counselor attractiveness. Bundga and Simonson (1973) reported that therapist self-disclosure facilitated client self-disclosure. Murphy and Strong (1972) found that interviewees perceived self-disclosing interviewers as more willing to be known as persons. This increased the interviewees' feelings of warmth, friendliness, and being understood. Tosi (1970) concluded that clients' ratings of the counseling relationship increased as counselor openness increased.

Self-disclosure is also a function of information content, target person, and sex of subject (Gitter and Black, 1976). Intimate information, as we would expect, is less readily disclosed than superficial information. Females reveal more information than males. High revealers tend to be more sincere than low revealers. Jourard (1959) stated that the amount of personal information an individual is willing to disclose is an index of the closeness of the therapeutic relationship.

Openness about feelings is related to accurately perceiving the verbal expression of feelings. Levy (1964) demonstrated that accurate identification of the verbalized feelings of others is related to the ability to recognize one's own feelings and be able to express them to others. This finding and the findings of several earlier studies obviously suggest that counselor behavior can be changed in a more effective direction. Lin (1973), for example, found that counselor genuineness was linearly related to self-disclosure. Confidence is a variable that through training can be increased. Delaney et al. (1969) noted that genuineness did indeed increase as a result of a practicum experience. Growth groups can also increase counselor insight, sensitivity, awareness, trust, and confidence which would correspondingly increase counselor genuineness and openness.

Dynamics of the Authentic Counseling Relationship Facilitative authenticity does not allow the counselor to hide behind a cloak or a disguise. The counselor is real and genuine in his or her being with the client. Life itself becomes real within the counseling fabric. As a result of the establishment of a relationship without the necessity for a mask, the client becomes more real and less phony. Perhaps for the first time the client can assess the true meaning of and reason for existence. The client in the search for identity can more clearly perceive personal values and will be more able to attain life choices through an increased comprehension of the reality of being in the world (Cottingham, 1966).

Authentic interaction suggests that the counselor be known by the client—not just professionally but personally. Verbal responses are a reflection of the counselor's inner feelings of care and concern. They are not programmed. While one can program the content of a verbal response, the care and concern of the counselor must be honest and genuine. Any attempt by the counselor at role playing will be recognized by the client, as will any insincere response. Peters and Farwell (1967) stated that "the counselor will perceive and sense a lack of genuineness, either through body language, tonal quality, or other subtle ways" (p. 238). The authenticity of the counselor is not superficial but is a reflection of a basic core of being.

Therapist transparency is a good term to describe non-superficial realness. Such behavior in the therapist provides the client with an important model. Counselor spontaneity and honesty genuinely communicated elicits and reinforces "kindred uncontrived behavior" (Jourard, 1964, p. 64). Essentially, "to the degree that the helpee can realize the authenticity of his helper, he can risk greater genuineness and authenticity himself" (Gazda, 1973, p. 50). In essence, the client sees a spontaneous, real, healthy individual and through the process of identification moves in that same direction. This may be a tedious process, for the counselor may be anxious about "being real," while the client may withdraw because of the presence of someone "real." But if the counselor continues to be authentic, and his/her transparency displays goodwill, the client will disclose so that the counselor may help.

An authentic interaction allows the counselor to eliminate any defenses or defensive behavior. The counselor is free to utilize all of his/her resources fully. The counselor is able to forget him/herself and, as a result, listens and responds more effectively. There is no need to expand energy to preserve a front.

The counselor is just as free to express feelings-in-the-moment as is the client. The counselor is open and, if he/she becomes tense, can say, "You are making me tense." Such openness is not only facilitative because of its genuine nature, but because it allows the client to see how others respond to him/her as a person. Arbuckle (1975) raises the issue that the "counselor must be free to feel his feelings during the counseling relationship, rather than bottling them up or presenting both to himself and to the client a blank face and pretending that he has no feelings" (p. 349). The counselor needs to be "aware of and honest with himself about the kinds of feelings the client is eliciting in him" (Hansen et al., 1977, p. 126). Meador and Rogers (1973) noted, "Congruence in the therapist's own inner self is his sensing of and reporting his own felt experiencing as he interacts in the relationship" (p. 139). Further, Rogers (1958) noted that the counselor "may need to talk about some of his own feelings (either to the client, or to a colleague or superior) if they are standing in the way" (pp. 133-134). The open expression of feelings "clears the air" and does not allow negative feelings to impede therapy.

An important principle to remember, however, is that therapy is not for the therapist. The concept of authenticity does not allow the counselor to dominate or indiscriminately reveal personal feelings. A certain degree of maturity and good judgment is called for. Belkin (1975) stated. "The counselor should not offer those feelings which he simply desires to offer but rather those which his experience and training tell him will be beneficial to the client" (p. 113). On one side of the coin we have the nonfacilitative, immature "closed" person, i.e., the counselor who is closed to feelings toward the client or, if the feelings are recognized, is unable to express them. On the other side of the coin we have the immature, nonfacilitative "open" counselor; this counselor does not exercise appropriate judgment regarding self-disclosure.

> The therapist's being freely and deeply himself in a non-exploitative relationship incorporates one critical qualification: when his only genuine responses are negative in regard to the second person, the therapist makes an effort to employ his responses constructively as a basis for further inquiry for the therapist, the client, and their relationship. [Carkhuff and Berenson, 1967, p. 29]

The counselor is a constructive agent, not a destructive one. He/She may challenge, but not intimidate; question, but not belittle; reveal, but not dominate.

A major emphasis in counseling, then, must be upon the genuine nature of the counselor, not upon gimmickry or "game-playing." Therapeutic behavior is reflective of the therapist and not a particular school of thought which he or she might represent. Fiedler's classic study in 1950 indicated that therapists generally agree on the most effective type of therapeutic relationship, and that theoretical differences are the result of poor communication between therapists of different schools (pp. 239-245). A "bag-of-tricks" is superficial when compared to the inner nature presented by the counselor.

> I find myself sometimes giving advice, lecturing, laughing, becoming angry, interpreting, telling my fantasies, asking questions—in short, doing whatever occurs to me during the therapeutic session in response to the other person. This change could mean either that I am growing as a person and as a therapist or else that, through lack of close supervision, I am 'losing' in discipline. [Jourard, 1964, p. 69]

As we mentioned earlier, it is important that the counselor's reactions have a therapeutic impact upon the client.

> I observe as I do during the whole period of therapy what genuine reactions his behavior causes in me. It might well

be the same adverse reaction which he often experiences from others, without being aware that he causes these reactions himself, at least partially. From sharing my personal reaction with him we can see more clearly the variety of reactions his behavior may bring about in others. My reaction and my willingness to reveal my reactions opens him up to a greater willingness to evaluate and communicate his own feelings. [Colm, 1965, p. 139]

The comment by Combs et al. (1969) still best reflects the nongenuine being of the poor helper.

We suspect a major problem of poor helpers is the fact that their methods are unauthentic, that is, they tend to be put on, contrived. As such, they can only be utilized so long as the helper keeps his mind on them. That, of course, is likely to be disastrous on two counts. In the first place it separates him from his client or student, and the message conveyed is likely to be that he is not 'with it,' is not really interested, or is a phony. Second, it is almost never possible to maintain attention to the 'right' method for very long. As a consequence the poor helper relapses frequently to what he believes or his previous experience has taught him, and so the method he is trying to use fails because of the tenuous, interrupted character of his use of it. [p. 76]

In times of stress the "real" person will come through. For example, we are sometimes surprised to know of someone who is both liked and disliked, i.e., liked by those who know him or her in a limited fashion, but disliked by others who know that person far more intimately. Obviously, the latter group has moved beyond dealing with the superficialities, which may well cover a multitude of sins. Another phenomenon which illustrates this is the teacher initially well-received by students, but who is intensely disliked by the end of the course. What we usually find is that once beyond the initial superficialities the teacher finds it difficult to disguise a less healthy inner self. We have seen the opposite, also. The person we pass in the hall may appear distant and aloof, and, yet, will turn out to be quite loving and facilitative.

Pitfalls, or the "Authentic" Trap There is one major (for lack of a better word) pitfall when the concept of authenticity is not clearly understood by the recipient. We have clearly stated that "method," "technique," or "skills" are secondary to the counselor as a person. This is often misinterpreted to mean that "skills" or "techniques" are not necessary. Obviously, this is not so. We recognize that certain skills are far more conducive to good human relations, and to the contrary, certain skills interrupt or prevent the establishment of a good relationship. What is required is for the counselor to try and develop an approach which is "personalized," i.e., to become the most highly trained and skilled professional that may be possible, and adapt and adjust those skills so that "I am comfortable" with them. It is our feeling, therefore, that one cannot be "Rogerian" except Carl Rogers, or "Ellisonian" except for Albert Ellis. We can learn, adapt, and modify but we can only be ourselves in the truly helping relationship.

On the other hand a counselor cannot be truly "authentic" without training or skills building. We cannot "deliver" ourselves if we do not know what we are capable of "delivering." We could have all the good intentions in the world, but counseling is more than just "good intentions."

Another problem associated with authentic being is counselor selection. A clear implication of this selection is that "facilitative" counselors are necessary if "genuineness" is to mean anything. *The last thing we want is an unhealthy counselor being genuine.* Counselor self-awareness needs to be emphasized in training programs as well as methodology.

Arnold (1962, pp. 185-192) believes that counselor education must be seen as "responsible self-government," for self-acceptance and openness to experience is a prerequisite to understanding and accepting others. Students can be educated to function at higher levels of facilitativeness. Therapists with experience come to be more freely, easily, and deeply involved in the therapeutic situation and, furthermore, didactic and experiential training encourages therapeutic personality change (Carkhuff and Berenson, 1967, p. 293). Such training encourages growth most effectively if it involves supervisors who themselves are functioning at a high degree of facilitation (Pierce and Schauble, 1970).

SUMMARY

A crucial dimension in counseling is the authentic being of the helper. While we recognize the importance of certain counselor behaviors, they have to be real. Such behaviors are not a "bag-of-tricks" designed to manipulate the client. Counselor behaviors reflect a "genuine" caring and concern. This is far more crucial than any technique which, if foreign to the inner nature of the counselor, will be easily seen through by the counselee. The importance of genuineness is reflected by Rogers (1962) when he stated. "I have sometimes wondered if this is the only quality which matters in a counseling relationship" (p. 156).

REFERENCES

Allen, Thomas W.
   1967 "Effectiveness of Counselor Trainees as a Function of Psychological Openness." *Journal of Counseling Psychology,* 14:35-40.

Altmann, H.A.
   1973 "Effects of Empathy, Warmth, and Genuineness in the Initial Counseling Interview." *Counselor Education and Supervision,* 12, 225-229.

Arbuckle, Dugald S.
   1967 *Counseling and Psychotherapy: An Overview.* New York: McGraw-Hill. Third Edition, 1975.

Arnold, Dwight L.
   1962 "Counselor Education as Responsible Self-Development." *Counselor Education and Supervision,* 1:185-192. Reprinted with permission of the publisher, American Personnel and Guidance Association, Washington, D.C.

Belkin, G. S.
   1975 *Practical Counseling in the Schools.* Dubuque, Iowa: William C. Brown Co.

Buber, M.
   1957 "Distance and Relation." *Psychiatry,* 20, 97-104.

Bundga, K. A., and Simonson, N. R.
   1973 "Therapist Self-Disclosure: Its Effects on Impressions of Therapist Willingness to Disclose." *Psychotherapy: Theory, Research, and Practice,* 10, 215-217.

Carkhuff, Robert R., and Berenson, Bernard G.
   1967 *Beyond Counseling and Therapy.* New York: Holt, Rinehart and Winston.

Coleman, James C.
   1974 *Abnormal Psychology and Modern Life.* Glenview, Ill.: Scott, Foresman and Company.

Colm, H.
   1965 "The Therapeutic Encounter." *Review of Existential Psychology and Psychiatry,* 5:137-159.

Combs, A. W., et al.
 1969 *Florida Studies in the Helping Professions.* Monograph No. 37. Gainesville: University of Florida Press.

Cottingham, Harold D.
 1966 "The Challenge of Authentic Behavior." *Personnel and Guidance Journal*, 45:328-336. Reprinted with permission of the publisher, American Personnel and Guidance Association, Washington, D.C.

Culberson, J. O.
 1975 "Effects of Low-level Counselor Functioning on Clients." *Counselor Education and Supervision*, 15, 34-38.

Cutler, R. L.
 1958 "Countertransference Effects in Psychotherapy." *Journal of Consulting Psychology*, 55, 349-356.

Delaney, D. J., Long, T. J., Masucci, M. J., and Moses, H. A.
 1969 "Skill Acquisition and Perception Change of Counselor Candidates During Practicum." *Counselor Education and Supervision*, 8, 273-282.

Demos, George D.
 1964 "Application of Certain Principles of Client-Centered Therapy." *Journal of Counseling Psychology*, 11:280-284.

Dies, R. R.
 1973 "Group Therapist Self-Disclosure: An Evaluation by Clients." *Journal of Counseling Psychology*, 20(4), 344-348.

Egan, G.
 1975 *The Skilled Helper.* Monterey, Ca.: Brooks/Cole.

Eisenberg, L., and Kanner, L.
 1956 "Early Infantile Autism: 1943-1955." *American Journal of Ortho Psychiatry*, 26:556-566.

Eisenberg, Sheldon, and Delaney, Daniel J.
 1977 *The Counseling Process.* Chicago: Rand McNally.

Fiedler, Fred E.
 1950 "The Concept of an Ideal Therapeutic Relationship." *Journal of Consulting Psychology*, 14:239-245.

Fischer, J., Paveza, G., Kickertz, N., Hubbard, L., and Grayston, S.
 1975 "The Relationship Between Theoretical Orientation and Therapists' Empathy, Warmth, and Genuineness." *Journal of Counseling Psychology*, 22(5), 399-403.

Gazda, G.
 1973 *Human Relations Development.* Boston: Allyn and Bacon.

Gendlin, E. T., and Geist, M.
 1962 *The Relationship of Therapist Congruence to Psychological Test Evaluations of Personality Change.* Wisconsin Psychiatric Institute, University of Wisconsin.

Giannandrea, V., and Murphy, K. C.
 1973 "Similarity Self-Disclosure and Return for a Second Interview." *Journal of Counseling Psychology*, 20(6), 545-548.

Gitter, A. G., and Black, H.
　1976　"Is Self-Disclosure Self-Revealing." *Journal of Counseling Psychology,* 23(4), 327-332.

Haley, J.
　1960　"Direct Study of Child-Parent Interaction III. Observation of the Family of the Schizophrenic." *American Journal of Orthopsychiatry,* 30, 460-467.

Halikides, G.
　1958　"An Experimental Study of Four Conditions Necessary for Therapeutic Change." Unpublished doctoral dissertation, University of Chicago.

Hansen, J.C., Stevic, R. R., and Warner, R. W.
　1977　*Counseling: Theory and Process.* Boston: Allyn and Bacon.

Hayden, B.
　1975　"Verbal and Therapeutic Styles of Experienced Therapists Who Differ in Peer-Rated Therapist Effectiveness." *Journal of Counseling Psychology,* 22(5), 384-389.

Hountras, Peter T., and Anderson, Dervyn L.
　1969　"Counselor Conditions for Self-Exploration of College Students." *Personnel and Guidance Journal,* 48:45-48. Reprinted with permission of the publisher, American Personnel and Guidance Association, Washington, D.C.

Johnson, David W., and Noonan, Patricia M.
　1972　"Effects of Acceptance and Reciprocation of Self-Disclosure on the Development of Trust." *Journal of Counseling Psychology,* 19(5), 411-416.

Jourard, S.
　1959　"Self-Disclosure and Other Cathexis." *Journal of Abnormal and Social Psychology,* 59, 428-431.

Jourard, Sidney M.
　1964　*The Transparent Self.* Princeton, N. J.: D. Van Nostrand. Copyright© 1964 by Litton Educational Publishing, Inc. Reprinted with permission of D. Van Nostrand.

Jourard, S. M., and Jaffe, P. E.
　1970　"Influence of an Interviewer's Disclosure on the Self-Disclosing Behavior of Interviewees." *Journal of Counseling Psychology,* 17(3), 252-257.

Jourard, S. M., and Whitman, A.
　1971　"The Fear that Cheats Us of Love." *Redbook,* October 1971, 154-160.

Kazan, Elia.
　1967　*The Arrangement.* New York: Stein and Day. Copyright© by Elia Kazan. Reprinted with permission of Stein and Day Publishers.

Laing, R. D., and Esterson, A.
　1964　*Sanity, Madness, and the Family.* London: Tavistock.

Lee, D. E., and Ehrlich, H. J.
  1971 "Beliefs About Self and Others: A Test of the Dogmatism Theory." *Psychological Reports,* 28, 919-922.

Levy, P. K.
  1964 "The Ability to Express and Perceive Vocal Communications to Feelings." In J. R. Donitz, ed. *The Communication of Emotional Meaning.* New York: McGraw-Hill.

Lin, Tien-Teh.
  1973 "Counseling Relationship as a Function of Counselor's Self-Confidence." *Journal of Counseling Psychology,* 20(4), 293-297.

Mark, J. C.
  1953 "The Attitudes of the Mothers of Male Schizophrenics Toward Child Behavior." *Journal of Abnormal and Social Psychology,* 48, 485-489.

Maslow, A.
  1953 "Creativity in Self-Actualizing People." In H. Anderson, ed. *Creativity and Its Cultivation.* New York: Harper and Row.

May, P. O., and Thompson, C. L.
  1973 "Perceived Levels of Self-Disclosure, Mental Health and Helpfulness of Group Leaders." *Journal of Counseling Psychology,* 20(4), 349-352.

Meador, B. D., and Rogers, C. R.
  1973 "Client-Centered Therapy." In *Current Psychotherapies,* R. Corsini, ed. Itasca, Ill.: F. E. Peacock.

Mezzano, J.
  1969 "A Note on Dogmatism and Counselor Effectiveness." *Counselor Education and Supervision,* 9, 64-65.

Murphy, K. C., and Strong, S. R.
  1972 "Some Effects of Similarity Self-Disclosures." *Journal of Counseling Psychology,* 19(2), 121-124.

Peters, Herman J., and Farwell, Gail F.
  1967 *Guidance: A Developmental Approach.* Chicago: Rand McNally.

Pierce, R. M., and Schauble, P. G.
  1970 "Graduate Training of Facilitative Counselors: The Effects of Individual Supervision." *Journal of Counseling Psychology,* 17:210-215.

Pietrofesa, John J., Clifton, Robert and Markman, Barry.
  1976 "Celebrity Interview." *Personnel and Guidance Journal,* 7(2), 3-8.

Rogers, Carl R.
  1958 "The Characteristics of a Helping Relationship." *Personnel and Guidance Journal* (1958) 37:6-16. In James F. Adams, *Counseling and Guidance: A Summary View.* New York: Macmillan, pp. 141-153.

  1962 "The Interpersonal Relationship: The Core of Guidance." *Harvard Educational Review* (1962) 32:416-429. In James F. Adams, *Counseling and Guidance: A Summary View.* New York: Macmillan, pp. 153-164.

Shapiro, J. G., Krauss, H., and Truax, C. B.
  1969 "Therapeutic Conditions and Disclosure Beyond the Therapeutic Encounter." *Journal of Counseling Psychology,* 16:290-294.

Singer, M.
    1961 "Patient-Family Similarities in Schizophrenia." *Archives of General Psychiatry,* 1961, 5, 120-126.
Spiritas, A. A., and Holmes, D. S.
    1971 "Effects of Models on Interview Responses." *Journal of Counseling Psychology,* 18(2), 217-220.
Staudenmeier, James J.
    1967 "Student Perceptions of Counselor Behavior Contributing to a Helping Relationship." *The School Counselor,* 15:113-117. Reprinted with permission of the publisher, American Personnel and Guidance Association, Washington, D.C.
Tosi, Donald J.
    1970 "Dogmatism Within the Counselor-Client Dyad." *Journal of Counseling Psychology,* 17(3), 284-288.
Truax, Charles B.
    1963 "Effective Ingredients in Psychotherapy: An Approach to Unraveling the Patient-Therapist Interaction." *Journal of Counseling Psychology,* 10:256-263.
Truax, Charles B., and Carkhuff, Robert R.
    1965 "Client and Therapist Transparency in the Psychotherapeutic Encounter." *Journal of Counseling Psychology,* 12:3-9.
    1967 *Toward Effective Counseling and Psychotherapy.* Chicago: Aldine.
Truax, C. B., Wittmer, J., and Wargo, D.
    1971 "Effects of Therapeutic Conditions of Accurate Empathy, Nonpossessive Warmth, and Genuineness on Hospitalized Patients During Group Therapy." *Journal of Clinical Psychology,* 27, 137-142.
Zigon, F., and Cannon, J. R.
    1974 "Processes and Outcomes of Group Discussions as Related to Leader Behaviors." *Journal of Educational Research,* 47, 253-257.

Chapter 7 Dimensions of Counselor Self-Actualization: The Fully Functioning Counselor

INTRODUCTION Maslow (1962b) defined self-actualization:

> as an episode, or a spurt in which the powers of the person come together in a particularly efficient and intensely enjoyable way, and in which he is more integrated and less split, more open for experience, more idiosyncratic, more perfectly expressive or spontaneous, or more fully functioning, more creative, more humorous, more ego-transcending, more independent of his lower needs, etc. He becomes in these episodes more truly himself, more perfectly actualizing his potentialities, closer to the core of his Being. [p. 91]

This chapter was originally presented in shortened form as a speech at the National Catholic Guidance Conference in Detroit (1969). The speech was later published in the *National Catholic Guidance Conference Journal*, 13 (1968): 28-32.

Certainly psychological well-being or counselor self-actualization is related to facilitation of counselor growth. In fact, a study by Foulds (1969, p. 132) found that personality characteristics associated with self-actualization were related to communication of respect or positive regard and also facilitative genuineness. While self-actualization and achievement are not directly related (Leib and Snyder, 1968, pp. 388-389), they are related secondarily through separate relationships with other variables (LeMay, 1969, pp. 582-583). Selfridge and Vander Kolk (1976) reported that there is a strong relationship between self-actualization and counselor effectiveness as perceived by clients.

Who is self-actualized? And can someone who is not self-actualized recognize someone who is? Can an individual who is trying to satisfy needs for esteem, for instance, truly recognize and accept another person who is not primarily engaged in such gratification? The writers think that ordinarily this would not be so. An individual who is basically interested in the satisfaction of esteem needs would think it odd that someone else is not also basically driven by such a need. A projection of "normality" would be made by the viewer, "For if you are not like me then it is you who is odd."

In some cases an individual may perceive another as a self-actualizing person, although the prime viewer is not yet self-actualized. This may be accomplished by an individual who has overcome or understands his/her own defense mechanisms and is most likely on the way to self-actualization him/herself.[1]

Counselors, since they are concerned with the self-actualization of their clients, must make a thorough study of themselves and their own progress towards self-actualization. They should understand their personality needs, the level at which they are functioning, and the defense mechanisms they use to preserve the self-concept. Personality hygienists could undoubtedly be helpful, but expense tends to make this impossible for most counselors except on a short-term basis. Yet there are a good many people who, through contact with facilitating persons, have been reopened and whose selves function well (Kelley, 1962, p. 18). It is suggested, therefore, that each potential counselor make a self-study before entering the field. Arnold (1962) writes, "A continuous

---

[1] Self-actualization is both a state and a process. It is not a static concept. In one sense, an individual may be self-actualized today and tomorrow move out of this state of self-actualization.

development of self and competencies which does not stop at the end of formal training is implied by this approach. If responsible self-development occurs in the formal training, then counselor development programs can build right on the former experiences" (p. 189). Such a study would be useful in achieving a positive relationship with, and an understanding of each counselee and would aid in helping the counselee become more fully functioning. Leonard (1960) states in regard to the counselor's growth in understanding his client:

> Progress is apt to be slow until the counselor gains insights into his own feelings and motivations as a client. This will call for a ceaseless, relentless self-evaluation on the part of the counselor in his continual, dynamic state of becoming ...It is, however, from this inner dimension that the counselor will gain his greatest impetus, as well as self-satisfaction. Only then will the counselor be stimulated continually to make progress on the road to becoming. Only then will the counselor make progress towards becoming a fully-functioning counselor in fact as well as name. [p. 37]

Frankl (1967) makes the point that self-actualization is a phenomenon which occurs not as a matter of direct intention—in fact, this may thwart such an occurrence—but can only be obtained as a side effect. He maintains, "That man can only actualize himself to the extent to which he fulfills meaning. Then self-actualization occurs spontaneously..." (p. 8). This in essence can be agreed with. However, the point should be made that people find meaning through answers to questions that they ask themselves. The sensitive individual, the one who consciously strives to find meaning in life, will actualize his/her potentialities. If someone raises questions about his/her existence in order to find such meaning, the achievement of self-actualization becomes more than simply a spontaneous occurrence.

It would be almost impossible to describe a self-actualizing counselor, but a beginning can be made by observing his/her behavior (Kelley, 1962, p. 17). The following discussion presents behavioral characteristics of self-actualizing counselors. It is not designed to be elaborate, but merely is a stimulant by which counselors can study and raise questions about themselves.

Emphasis on Experience The self-actualizing counselor tends to stress the concept of identity and experience of identity in human nature. He/She emphasizes experiential knowledge rather than systems of concepts or abstract categories, and is open to his/her own experiences, rather than being closed or defensive. There is little concern with preservation of previously formulated ideas or attitudes. The realization is present that the counselor is a growing organism—one that continually assimilates and incorporates experience into one's own being. Such an individual is not easily threatened, for threat brings forth a narrowing of the perceptual field, a defensive stance, and a distortion of reality. To be open means to allow for the possibility of rediscovery, stimulation, reconception, and even rebirth. This individual is better able to understand him/herself or another being. He/She tries to perceive any situation as the client sees it, rather than as an individual who is primarily concerned with placing a value judgment on the behavior of another person.

Client: I haven't thought ahead, no.
Counselor: Haven't had time to think?
Client: I have enough trouble just taking each day as it comes, and no time to think ahead.
Counselor: Every day is a pretty big thing.
Client: A pretty big mess. Now listen, I realize you have to have a high school education to get a job, and it doesn't seem to bother me. It bothers me, but I don't seem to want to do anything about it.
Counselor: You feel that not doing something about it is your problem?
Client: It's part of it I guess. I don't actually know my problem. Maybe I'm nuts.
Counselor: What would make you think that?
Client: I don't know. I just . . . I realize everything but . . . when I'm in my principal's office I'll promise anything under the sun, you know, and then I get outside and tell myself, "I hate school."
Counselor: You really feel you hate it?
Client: I guess that's what you'd call it—I hate it.
Counselor: It really tears you up, doesn't it?

Client: Yeah. But all through elementary school and junior high, I had A's and B's—you know, straight through.
Counselor: You did real well.
Client: I started dropping about the ninth grade, and my grades dropped say one level each. And I got at Tech High and boy . . . but it's my own fault. It's not that the work's too hard or anything.
Counselor: You just can't seem to get interested in putting your nose to the grindstone.
Client: That's right. It just doesn't seem to interest me, or I don't seem to want to do it.
Counselor: You don't really know why you're avoiding the issue and skipping out on it, huh?
Client: No, I don't. I dropped chemistry earlier, you know, thought maybe that would help me out so I'd have more time for the other subjects, but . . . I was in, let's see, it was I believe a Wednesday, I spent all day with my counselor and the assistant principal; my mother came down. I promised them no more skipping; I'd do my work and try and catch up. The Monday after that I skipped school.
Counselor: Did it bother you to do this?
Client: At the time it doesn't. When I think about how asinine it is, it does.

Rogers (1961) feels:

> As you might expect, this increasing ability to be open to experience makes him far more realistic in dealing with new people, new situations, new problems. It means that his beliefs are not rigid, that he can tolerate ambiguity. He can receive much conflicting evidence without forcing closure upon the situation. This openness of awareness to what exists at this moment in oneself and in the situation is, I believe, an important element in the description of the person who emerges from therapy. [pp. 115-116]

Rejection of Manipulation The effective counselor does not manipulate a client to support a particular philosophy of counseling, but utilizes those measures which are most helpful in achieving self-actualization in that client. Dreyfus (1964) says, "The counselor must expose himself, and, therefore, cannot maintain the scientific objective attitude of the physical scientist. He cannot view the client as an object to be manipulated, exploited and explored" (p. 117). Jourard (1964) states that counselees:

> Come to us because they have become so estranged from their real selves that they are incapable of making these known to their associates in life. I don't see how we can reacquaint our patients with their real selves by striving to subject them to subtle manipulations ... [p. 74]

Manipulation tends to be countered with manipulation. What if this happens in the counseling relationship?

The counselor (or any individual, for that matter) does violence to him/herself when he/she tries to manipulate another. For the process is tantamount to selling one's soul. Harris (1968) editorializes: "That every time we use a person for our own purpose, ignoring his needs, we diminish ourselves more than we diminish him, for his is a wound that can heal, while ours is an amputation that cannot grow back" (p. 7A).

In the following counseling excerpt, the counselee broaches rather cautiously the fact that he has withdrawn from school. The counselor could well have attempted to manipulate him into enrolling once again. Instead, the behavior of the counselor resulted in the counselee making his own decision.

> *Counselor:* What brought you down here?
> *Client:* I don't ... I skip school all the time.
> *Counselor:* You skip school?
> *Client:* Yeah, I go to Tech High; you know that, don't you? I know you need an education in this world, you know, to get any kind of job. Still I start off for school and something happens and I just don't make it. I go somewhere else—downtown usually.
> *Counselor:* You feel that skipping school isn't too good?
> *Client:* No, not at all. And I quit today.

Counselor: You decided to quit school today?
Client: Yeah.
Counselor: Do you feel this was good or bad?
Client: Bad, but I figured, you know, Tech has pretty high standards for high school. I figured I might have a higher potential than somebody who tried to get into Tech, but it might be better for them to go because they'd want to learn and they'd try; and I don't try. And I don't think I should just go and take up space that someone else would rather have than I would.
Counselor: It's wrong to sit there and occupy a place?
Client: Yeah.
Counselor: Quitting school today, is it going to help other people or yourself?
Client: It's not going to help me; I hope it helps somebody else.
Counselor: Well, you feel that this is a real problem, don't you?
Client: Yeah.
Counselor: What do you feel you can do about it?
Client: I haven't any idea. I don't know what I'm doing.
Counselor: Too many things going wrong all at once, then?
Client: Yeah.
Counselor: You haven't done too well.
Client: No, I haven't. But I feel it's my own fault because I don't spend enough time on my homework. Sometimes I don't even do it. Sometimes I don't even bring the books home. I mean it's no fault of the school; it's just my own fault. But I don't know what's happening. You know, I could probably do the work. You have to read and study and all that stuff, and I realize that, but I don't do it. I don't know what in the heck's goin' on.
Counselor: You really don't understand why you can't get organized, huh?

> *Client:* No. I wasn't even going to come here today to be truthful with you; I wasn't. I figured maybe you could help me; I need it.
>
> *Counselor:* Well, I'm here to help. Anything that I can do. Maybe just talking will help, you know, do some thinking a little bit about it. Have you been thinking ahead at all? Where are you going?

Avoidance of Counselee Classification Basic to the principle of "accepting the counselee" is the idea that the counselor be able to listen to the client in a receiving way; a way that does not imply that the counselor would like to hear certain things. Some counselors give the impression that there is a right and a wrong statement to be made at a certain time. This cannot be done in a true counseling situation in which the client is trying to clarify the "real self." The client must be seen as a human being by the counselor, not as a truant or a disciplinary problem. To perceive an individual as one of a class is in fact to say, "You are just like all the rest." The client, however, is not like all the rest. He/She is inherently different from all the rest. In fact, the one sure assumption the counselor can make is that this client differs from all other individuals in the counselor's past. Maslow (1962b) proposes that the good counselor is able to perceive each person in his/her own right, without the urge to "taxonomize, rubricize, classify, and pigeonhole" (p. 214). Colm (1965) writes that, "One such technique which I have found fruitful is to listen and try to observe the patient's behavior and his symptoms, forgetting preconceived diagnostic patterns which so often lead us to overlook or overstress factors or see the patient in terms of a general pattern rather than how he is" (p. 138).

Evans, the central character of Kazan's *The Arrangement* (1967) says, "For the first time in my life I was able to feel close to people because for the first time I didn't make those judgments-in-advance, and pigeon-holings-out-of-hand, that had made it impossible for me in the past to actually know anyone" (p. 479). A satisfactory counseling relationship cannot be established based upon such classification. If the reader doubts this, just say to an adolescent with a problem, "All teenagers have a very similar problem to yours." That adolescent may never return to the counseling relationship again unless it is based on collusion. The process of labeling or classifying is rejected rather vividly in the following dialogue.

Client: I was skipping school for a while there. The reason I was skipping was not that I disliked school; I do like the teachers and the friends, but I really thought it was useless and a waste. I've been getting A's and all sorts of crud until ninth grade. I'm in tenth grade now and it seemed like I never did anything. I still got A's. So everyone went around and said, "Wow, you're so smart." I mean it's not the grading system and stuff; it's just that I think it's so ridiculous. You can't judge someone's intelligence on whether you get an A or E.

Counselor: You don't like the label that they put on you because you got all A's.

Client: Yeah! Right! They naturally assumed that just because she got an A, she can accept more responsibility. Oh, not that I mind accepting more responsibility. They decided others couldn't accept the same amount of responsibility. And so they degraded the potential of others who grasp things as quickly. I don't feel that is very fair. Like this year, it was just the same thing. In English I wouldn't even have to go and I got B's. I made it to the final and I think I answered a few questions on it. I was late for the final, too, and I had a C which is ridiculous. I mean I didn't deserve a C for nothing.

Counselor: Are you saying that because they know you have the potential, they give you the grade anyway?

Client: They just gave it. I don't care how I got a C or a B or E, it's just ridiculous. It just shows you how stupid the grading system is. I could do nothing and get a C. I could do just nothing.

The effective counselor views people as open-ended. Openness is stressed in all encounters with others. An open counselor would find it difficult to approach all counselees from the point of view that they are attempting to compensate for early childhood feelings of inferiority. The facilitator has a positive rather than negative view of others.

> It makes a great deal of difference whether helpers perceive their clients as able or unable. If a counselor, teacher, or priest does not regard his clients as able, he can hardly permit them, let them, or trust them to act on their own; to do so would be a violation of responsibility. Apparently, effective helpers tend to see the persons they work with in essentially positive ways as dependable, friendly, and worthy people. [Combs et al., 1969, pp. 72-73]

Self-Expression The self-actualizing counselor is able to express him/herself freely, without feeling guilty or anxious about each statement. The counselor's self-expression must be true to the basic core of his/her self-concept, because if denial or suppression dominates the individual, he/she will get "sick." When hostilities or frustrations arise in the environment, the self-actualizing person can voice his/her anger.

The following session developed with the counselee describing his "trying" times in a science teacher's class. The counselor probed at the feeling level, but the counselee again and again attempted to bring the session to a head by asking for a transfer to another class. Finally, frustrated, the counselor responded:

> *Counselor:* You know, Paul, I'm starting to feel a little bit uncomfortable—in fact, a little angry. I'm not sure, but I have the feeling you're not telling the complete truth about Mrs. Smith. I know her, and it just doesn't sound like her.
> *Client:* [*Silence*]
> *Counselor:* Your silence indicates to me I may be right.
> *Client:* I had a feeling you'd take the teacher's side.
> *Counselor:* You're getting me angry again by trying to put me on the defensive.
> *Client:* [*Silence*]

This session was finally terminated. The counselee left looking indignant. Several weeks later he returned, stated he was now doing much better in science, and after much hesitation, apologized. He admitted that the real motive behind his original request for a transfer was to be in his girl's class.

Satisfaction of Needs Personality needs have an obvious influence upon perception. Need satisfaction generally is related to positive mental health, while deprivation narrows and distorts perception. This, of course, does not imply a total absence of frustration, for this is equally undesirable. Some frustration experiences are necessary in order to build tolerance. Counselor behavior during counseling is influenced by the counselor's need pattern. It is essential, then, for "counselors to be cognizant of their own needs, since they would thus be more knowledgeable of the determinants of their counseling behaviors" (Loesch and Weikel, 1976, p. 59). The more effective counselor has satisfied his/her viscerogenic and psychogenic needs and is engaged in the satisfaction of his/her need for "self-actualization." Such a counselor does not view a counselee as a means of satisfying a more basic need, e.g., viewing the counselee as a sex object or as a way to achieve esteem in the eyes of the administrator. He/She wants to help the counselee because the counselee is a human being who is seeking to move toward self-actualization. The person who has satisfied his/her basic needs is less dependent on others and is more self-directing. He/She enjoys interacting with people, but also treasures moments of solitary meditation.

Being as Well as Becoming The self-actualizing counselor is interested in being—in living every moment as fully as possible—as well as becoming. He/She needs to confront him/herself honestly, for truth is found in the experiencing of oneself. The counselor's past is only important as it affects him/her now, and he is able to transcend that past. He/She wants to *be* a counselor, then, a person engaged in the enterprise of helping others to *be* more fully functioning.

Being does not imply nongrowth, lack of movement, or stagnation of the individual. In fact, the opposite is true. Being allows one to be adaptable, and nonpredictable in one's behavior, a pulsating, vibrant organism. Leonard (1968) suggests "only through being in the sense of becoming will the counselor be able continually to adjust to the changing demands of his counselees, his society, and his educational-occupational world" (p. 33). Maslow (1962a) states further, "One for whom no future exists is reduced to the concrete, to hopelessness, to emptiness. For him, time must be endlessly 'filled.' Striving, the usual organizer of most activity, when lost, leaves the person unorganized and unintegrated" (p. 48).

Concern with Professionalization The self-actualizing counselor is concerned with professional standards. He/She expresses dismay at an individual who brings discredit to the profession, for he/she realizes that discreditation to the profession also brings discreditation to him/herself. He/She recognizes that in order to keep his/her desire for esteem satisfied, such a possibility must be avoided. Various professional activities are engaged in, not only to aid in the self-actualization of clients, but to maintain the high professional standards of the counseling field, so that other counselors may find satisfaction of their need for esteem.

Playing the Role of Counselor Jourard (1964) feels that:

> Roles are inescapable. They must be played or else the social system will not work. A role by definition is a repertoire of behavior patterns which must be rattled off in appropriate contexts, and all behavior which is irrelevant to the role must be suppressed. But what we often forget is the fact that it is a person who is playing the role. This person has a self, or I should say he is a self. All too often the roles that a person plays do not do justice to all of his self. [p. 22]

Sometimes one may find counselors playing the role of a counselor. These are people who unconsciously are impersonating what they feel the role of the counselor should be. They may do so out of simple insecurities' or, more basic, because they refuse to acknowledge the real self. Such individuals can never be self-actualized or effective counselors. They are pretending to be what they are, and their actions are not spontaneous, but rather well thought out. They frequently ask the question, "Is this what is expected of me in this situation?" These counselors have a nebulous self-concept, since they are forcing themselves into roles. The counselor who uses such action as a masquerade becomes "not real" anymore. One of the basic functions of the existentialist counselor is to provide a setting in which as little, as possible impedes the counselee's capacity to discover him/herself (Laing, 1962). Role playing, however, by the counselor does interfere with his/her relationship with the client since it is not a "true" relationship. The client, if he/she reacts, is reacting to a false self rather than the real self of the counselor. Most sensitive counselees can easily notice the signs of a "role playing" counselor, e.g., the overly cheerful greeting, the enthusiastic handshake and the phony backslap. Blocher (1966) writes, "The counselor who tries deliberately to be 'reassuring or supportive' today and 'objective and analytical' tomorrow is obviously playing a set of parts for the client's benefit and, no matter what his artistry as an actor will eventually be recognized as an actor and nothing more" (p. 145). In an effective counseling relationship, the client must see the counselor as a real person, not as one playing at a role. What a counselee needs as much as anything else is a spontaneous individual to react to, an individual who is going to be honest. The "role playing" counselor is basically dishonest, not only to others, but also to him/herself.

Some "role playing" counselors appear to be successful in their relationship with clients. This success, however, is based on collusion and results in a sterile and artificial counseling atmosphere. Laing (1962) defines collusion as mutual self-deception. In other words, one individual says to the other, "You recognize my false-self system or role and I will recognize yours." This may involve the counselor substantiating the false role of the counselee as "good and dutiful" while the counselee supports the counselor in his/her false role. Both leave the counseling relationship apparently satisfied, but it is an empty satisfaction.

Lack of Self-Consciousness The self-actualizing counselor is not self-centered, but is able to concentrate on the stimuli in the environment. Maslow (1962a) states: "The achievement of self-actualization (in the sense of autonomy) paradoxically makes more possible the transcendence of self, and of self-consciousness and of selfishness. It makes it easier for the person to be homonymous, i.e., to merge himself as a part in a larger whole than himself" (p. 47). This enables the counselor to become absorbed in the problems that face him/her and to be sensitive to cues that the self-involved individual cannot perceive. Such a counselor can penetrate to the core or essence of another person. He/She is able to autonomously work on people for all need satisfaction, as does the "other-directed" individual.

Willingness to Accept Knowledge In order to be fully functioning, the counselor must be willing to accept knowledge about the environment, other people, and him/herself. He/she does not view new information and scientific advances as a threat, and is flexible and able to adjust to a new perception of things. He/She aids others in questioning and exploring new areas of information, and avoids punishing others who question his/her value judgments and perceptual field. There is a respect for the right of others to dissent. Knowledge implies action in two ways. First, knowledge is acquired through interaction with the world and second, one's knowledge is reflected through one's behavior in the world. Skinner (1957) stated, "Men act upon the world, and change it, and are changed in turn by the consequences of their action" (p. 1).

Interestingly, counselor propensity for change is related to the facilitative dimensions they can provide. Counselors providing higher levels of facilitativeness are themselves more open to personal change (Passons and Dey, 1972).

There is not only an openness and acceptance of new knowledge present in the self-actualizing person, but such a person also interacts with, reacts to, and uses this knowledge in a creative way. He/She can go beyond traditional approaches to solving traditional problems. He/She has insights which generally do not occur to others, and is imaginative—at times a dreamer—but because of this, more adequate.

Counselor Moral Development   An interesting application of the work of Lawrence Kohlberg in moral development might be made to counselor functioning. Kohlberg (1975) posits that moral development is reflected by progress through six developmental stages. Each stage (1) is age-related, (2) occurs in an invariant sequence, and (3) is qualitatively different from and more comprehensive than the preceding stage. Kohlberg conceives of moral development as a reflection of the cognitive processes and as reflected by the reasoning for a behavior rather than by the behavior itself. The six stages are as follows:

>   **Preconventional Level**
>   *Stage 1*—At this stage obedience to an authority figure because of a fear of punishment is important. Behavior is viewed in light of possible physical consequences, e.g., don't smoke because the principal will catch you and paddle you. The stage one person believes that he/she is dominated from outside forces. This stage reflects a

"might makes right" or "survival of the fittest" orientation. Stage one behavior is designed to avoid physical punishment.

Stage 2—At stage two there is great concern with self-satisfaction and one's own needs. The needs of others are considered, but only as they might benefit "me." Some business-like transactions occur at this stage, e.g., the kickback. "Looking out for number one" is important. Instrumental hedonism may be seen in a stage two person.

Conventional Level

Stage 3—At stage three there is much conformity to the beliefs and expectations of others. The idea is to gain acceptance, i.e., to be a "good boy or girl." The "other-directed" person would reflect this type of thinking. Stereotypes are important, as are fixed conventional ways of behavior.

Stage 4—Duty and honor is important at this moral stage. It is felt that laws need to be upheld in order to preserve the social structure. A stable civil and criminal law code is sought with a rather rigid application of these laws.

Post-Conventional Level

Stage 5—There is a legal orientation at this stage with a social contract emphasis. Laws are not viewed as absolutes, but as something to be decided upon by the society. "Laws are made to be changed," but they are changed within the legal structure designed to achieve such change. Law is a matter, then, of agreement. Principled thought is important at stage five in the development of various laws.

Stage 6—At stage six one's conscience determines what is right or wrong. What is right is grounded in ethical principles that are general and universal, e.g., justice and equality for all. Such principles are viewed as superior to a given law. Human dignity is important at stage six.

What are the implications of the preceding for counseling? There are probably several, but they all point to the following generalizations. First, it is conceived that individuals move from one stage to the next higher stage by coming into contact with thinking reflective of that stage. Moral development proceeds as a result of human interaction. The relationship between the counselor and client thus becomes a vehicle to encourage moral growth. Second, it is rather obvious that a counselor at a lower stage of development would not be able to provide an atmosphere conducive to client growth. For example, a stage three counselor would not allow for a client decision which would go against the grain of popular thought, while a stage four counselor could not tolerate an action which would conflict with established rules or regulations. An effective counselor could help to create counseling discussions which would foster moral development. Such discussions would best facilitate growth in others if conducted by stage five or six counselors. Thus, it is imperative that counselors reflect higher stages of moral thought.

Commitment As self-actualizing counselors: we must not only be aware and sensitive, but we must be committed to do away with any behavior which dehumanizes the human being. We must get involved. Not only must we be responsible, professional counselors, but we have to go beyond performing adequately in our professional roles. We have a greater responsibility, a responsibility to prevent the dehumanization of people.

We talk about the "disadvantaged," usually in terms of economic deprivation, when in fact, the disadvantaged person is not necessarily the poor person or the person who lives in the inner city. The disadvantaged person may be the one who has two cars, has a well-paying job, has two bathrooms, and has an education; yet he/she does nothing to combat injustices to other humans, and in fact, may perpetuate such attitudes simply by noncommittal attitudes or by prejudices.

Commitment means *action.* Not a profound word, but it is a word that can make a difference in the future. A counselor once told a counselee who was indecisive, "Get off the pot." We, in the helping professions, ought to "get off the pot" and do something about those things which we philosophize so well.

COUNSELORS AS MODELS Healthy counselor attributes are important, for increased recognition is being given to the fact that the counselor serves as a model for the client. We find that as counseling progresses the client not only imitates specific counselor behaviors such as attending posture, but also modes of social interaction. Obviously, these modes of interaction are reflective of deeper philosophical and conceptual beliefs of humanness (as might even the simple behavioral posture of leaning forward to listen attentively to another person). If we accept the fact that modeling is an effective procedure to achieve change in the client, the client needs to be confronted with characteristics conducive to health and spiritual well-being.

SUMMARY

Emphasis should be placed by each counselor upon the evaluation of his/her effort to achieve self-actualization. By doing so, he/she will be better able to help others in the process of self-actualization. Self-actualization is a goal toward which many individuals move, but few achieve. It might be obtained through a willingness to accept knowledge, by concern over being as well as becoming, and by a sense of awareness and commitment to one's values and beliefs. Yet, the first step of self-actualization involves an assessment of where one is. This should then provide a stimulus for self-growth.

REFERENCES

Arnold, Dwight L.
    1962 "Counselor Education as Responsible Self-Development." *Counselor Education and Supervision,* 1:185-192.

Blocher, D. H.
    1966 *Developmental Counseling.* New York: The Ronald Press. Copyright © 1966, The Ronald Press Company, New York.

Colm, H.
    1965 "The Therapeutic Encounter." *Review of Existential Psychology and Psychiatry,* 5:137-159.

Combs, A. W., et al.
    1969 *Florida Studies in the Helping Professions.* Monograph No. 37. Gainesville· University of Florida Press.

Dreyfus, Edward.
    1964 "The Counselor and Existentialism." *Personnel and Guidance Journal,* 43:117. Reprinted with permission of the publisher, American Personnel and Guidance Association, Washington, D.C.

Foulds, Melvin L.
    1969 "Self-Actualization and the Communication of Facilitative Conditions During Counseling." *Journal of Counseling Psychology,* 16:132-136.

Frankl, Viktor E.
1967 *Psychotherapy and Existentialism:* Selected Papers on Logotherapy. New York: Simon and Schuster.

Harris, Sydney J.
1968 "Resisting the Easier Path." *Miami Herald,* No. 152. April 30, p. 7A. Reprinted by permission of Sydney J. Harris and Publishers-Hall Syndicate.

Jourard, Sidney.
1964 *The Transparent Self.* Princeton, N.J.: D. Van Nostrand. Revised edition, 1971.

Kazan, E.
1967 *The Arrangement.* New York: Stein and Day. Copyright© 1967 by Elia Kazan. Reprinted with permission of Stein and Day Publishers.

Kelley, E. C.
1962 "The Fully-Functioning Self." In Association for Supervision and Curriculum Development. *Perceiving, Behaving, Becoming.* Washington, D.C.: National Education Association, pp. 9-20.

Kohlberg, L.
1975 "The Cognitive-Developmental Approach to Moral Development." *Phi Delta Kappan,* 56:670.

Laing, R. D.
1962 *The Self and Others.* Chicago: Quadrangle Books.

Leib, J. W., and Snyder, W. U.
1968 "Achievement and Positive Mental Health." *Journal of Counseling Psychology,* 15:388-389.

LeMay, M. L.
1969 " Self-Actualization and College Achievement at Three Ability Levels." *Journal of Counseling Psychology,* 16:582-583.

Leonard, George E.
1968 "Counselor-Being?" *National Catholic Guidance Conference Journal,* 13:33-38.

Loesch, L. C., and Weikel, W. J.
1976 "Perceived and Measured Needs Levels of Counselor Education Students." *Counselor Education and Supervision,* 16:59-65.

Maslow, A. H.
1962a "Some Basic Propositions of a Growth and Self-Actualization Psychology." In Association for Supervision and Curriculum Development. *Perceiving, Behaving, Becoming.* Washington, D.C.: National Education Association, pp. 34-50.

1962b *Toward a Psychology of Being.* Princeton, N.J.: D. Van Nostrand. Copyright© 1962 by Litton Educational Publishing, Inc. By permission of D. Van Nostrand.

Passons, W. R., and Dey, G. R.
1972 "Counselor Candidate Personal Change and the Communication of

Facilitative Dimensions." *Counselor Education and Supervision,* 12:57-62.

Rogers, C. R.
   1961 *On Becoming A Person.* Boston: Houghton Mifflin.

Selfridge, F. F., and Vander Kolk, C.
   1976 "Correlates of Counselor Self-Actualization and Client-Perceived Facilitativeness." *Counselor Education and Supervision,* 15:189-94.

Skinner, B. F.
   1957 Verbal Behavior. New York: Appleton-Century-Crofts, Educational Division, Meredith Corporation.

Appendix

Counseling Practicum Handbook

The *Counseling Practicum Handbook* has been developed over the years by the authors at the Wayne State University Counseling Laboratory. It is designed to communicate to the counselor-candidate the purposes and procedures of the *Practicum*. Consequently, some of the procedures may not apply to the *Practicum* as it operates at other colleges and universities.

At the end of the *Handbook* are several information resources which should prove helpful to both student and instructor.

THE COUNSELING PRACTICUM As counseling has moved toward full acceptance as a profession, training programs have begun to focus on the importance of, and necessity for, supervised practice in counseling. Nevertheless, only recently has the formal practicum experience been established as a requirement by institutional programs and by various certification agencies. The graduate program of counselor education should include supervised practice in counseling to help effect the change of a counselor-candidate to an independently functioning counselor. The counseling practicum is included in this area as is the guidance and counseling internship. Both provide the opportunity for counselor-candidates to apply their theoretical background with practical skills in counseling situations.

The counseling practicum consists of actual supervised counseling experience. As a counselor-candidate, you will handle real counseling cases under systematic supervision and evaluation. We feel the practicum must be a growth experience for you. As such, it represents the major practical experience in a program of counselor education. The program includes those functions associated with handling actual counseling cases: counseling with students, consulting occasionally with parents, recording interviews, listening to taped interviews, wiriting summary reports, and reacting to observation both in individual conferences and in small group sessions.

The meaning of the practicum experience will vary according to the interpretation of your needs. Students usually find the practicum affords them an opportunity to synthesize the more or less fragmented phases of academic work and the actual problems of individual clients. In this way, your potential professional knowledge and skill will be centered not on purely academic ends, but upon the development of the client.

It has been said that preparation for counseling involves three kinds of learning: (1) information and concepts, (2) skills, and (3) professional role and self-development. As Arnold[1] puts it:

> The third is the most important . . . (for) without the third the counselor will remain a mechanic who will often turn from effective counseling and human relations to bury himself in testing, record keeping, and the minutiae of his work. With the third developed, he will tend to find his weaknesses in the other two and correct them. Without it his insecurities will grow or at least will not diminish.

[1] Dwight L. Arnold. "Counselor Education as Responsible Self-Development." *Counselor Education and Supervision*, 1 (1962): 187.

In accordance with the acceptance of the philosophy underlying this statement, counselor-supervisors should emphasize all areas of professional development with particular emphasis upon giving the candidate the opportunity to progress in self development.

Often the prospective counselor will look for "the right way" of handling a particular situation, "the correct words" to say to a counselee, or "the best thing to do" when confronted with a problem. Let it be said quickly that there are few easy ways to approach most situations. If there were, counseling would not be a matter of considered judgment, a characteristic that makes counseling a profession. Each counselee is an individual and needs to function as such. A technique or approach that may be appropriate for one counselor, then, might be ineffective, or even damaging, for another.

Throughout your practicum experience, it might be well to keep the following question in mind:

"Am I developing a counseling role which is

... compatible with my own personal makeup and beliefs?"

... compatible with general principles of counseling practice?"

... compatible with the role I will wish to practice in the future?"

Supervisors try not to force any particular role upon the counselor. What they attempt to do is to help you look at yourself as a counselor and examine your counseling practices, all toward the end of helping you to become more effective.

THE COUNSELING INTERVIEW The interview is the vehicle of counseling. As such, it conveys to the participants information about the questions, needs and characteristics of the counselee *and* the attitudes and competencies of the counselor. It is well to remember, though that the interview is but the means for communication and not communication per se. Consequently, how the counselor communicates his/her understanding and acceptance—verbally and nonverbally—is of critical importance. We can conceive of counseling without psychometrics, occupational briefs, or educational bulletins, but we cannot think of it without the face-to-face meeting of counselor and counselee.

Counseling, although a cooperative process involving both counselor and counselee, must center around the needs and purposes of the counselee. The counselee may be in need of information: understanding, a helping hand, or training in skills of learning, problem solving, or decision making. He/She may wish to define and clarify goals and values or seek an opportunity to think. Usually *several* needs are present in the counselee and these will change during counseling.

The counseling interview provides an opportunity for the counselor to understand the counselee. The improvement in the counselee's self-understanding is directly related to the counselor's understanding of the client. In order for this growth in counselor understanding to be facilitated, the focus of the interview must remain on the counselee.

What does keeping the focus on the counselee mean in actual practice? Simply, that emphasis must be kept continually on the counselee's needs and interests, not on what the counselor may wish to discuss or about which he/she may want information. A counselor must learn how to listen creatively—as Reik put it, with a "third ear." Only in this fashion can the counselor begin to see the counselee's world through his/her eyes. For example, the counselee may mention that he/she is interested in a particular career. It is more important for the counselor to understand *how* that career is perceived or how the counselee sees him/herself in that career than to immediately correct any possible misconceptions the client may have about the occupation. Following are several instances where the focus during the interviews has been shifted to what the counselor considers important and not on what the counselee is trying to say.

1. *Counselee:* "My parents never let me go out at night."
   Counselor: "Yes, but don't you think they have good reasons?"
2. *Counselee:* "I'd like to become a nurse someday."
   Counselor: "What do you know about nursing?"
3. *Counselee:* "I really like to go to the school dances."
   Counselor: "What else do you do around school?"
4. *Counselee:* "I'd like to leave home if I could."
   Counselor: "Where would you go?"
5. *Counselee:* "There's nobody I could really say is my friend."
   Counselor: "I'm sure that a nice boy like you has many friends."

6. *Counselee:* "I've just got to go to college."
   Counselor: "Well, according to these tests, you certainly could succeed."

In each of the above cases, the counselor—although superficially "staying with" the topic—has changed the direction of the conversation to something that he/she considers either pertinent or important.

One of the greatest dangers for either the beginning or practicing counselor is that of falling into a rigid pattern of responding to clients in terms of predetermined needs. Often the counselor will, upon reading an application for counseling, make a judgment that will later prove to be erroneous.

Sensitivity to what the counselee is saying is a skill that can be acquired by most well-adjusted persons. As the saying goes, "Counselors are made, not born." And in the practicum the counselor will find him/herself growing in this sensitivity. The counselor will, no doubt, be encouraged to "stay with" the counselee sometime during the practicum. In short, this will refer to talking about what the client wishes to talk about. Ask yourself, "What is he/she trying to tell me?" *not* "What other information do I need to reach a decision?"

COUNSELING STYLE   Counselors often refer to counseling style in terms of being "directive," "nondirective," "Rogerian," "client-centered," "eclectic," and the like.

A number of research studies that have been conducted, however, indicate that counselors usually adopt a style that is harmonious with their personal makeup and with which they can feel comfortable. If so, then the attempt to "label" or effect a particular counseling approach serves little practical purpose. It would seem much more constructive to evaluate counseling in terms of understanding and progress than to attempt to assess whether a counselor is utilizing a particular approach. Consequently, the counselor should look upon the practicum experience as an opportunity to examine and reexamine his/her own philosophy of counseling. "Just what do I believe?" and "Am I practicing what I preach?" are questions you should be considering as you review your counseling.

It would seem of value to review several principles of counseling with which counseling theorists agree. To begin with, all would agree that counseling is, and must be, a learning experience for the counselee. (It is a truism that often counseling becomes a learning experience for the counselor as well, but that is not the primary purpose.) The question then becomes, how can we help create conditions that will facilitate learning? Part of the answer lies in the counselor's attitude. It has been demonstrated that an attitude of unconditional warmth and acceptance on the part of the counselor will help achieve a counselee learning process. Perhaps adapting Voltaire's famous statement will illustrate an appropriate mindset for the counselor, "I may not agree with what you say, do, or want to do; but here I will help you to talk about what may concern you in hopes of helping you to become more self-sufficient." This statement could also convey the idea of a counseling atmosphere, which should be one of permissiveness and respect. Permissive in the sense that the counselee determines what he/she wishes to do; respectful in regard to the counselor understanding the counselee's right to make his/her own decisions. *No counseling theorist approves of the counselor making decisions for the counselee,* because we do not know what is best for others. Many writers would support the idea that a counselor must accept responsibility for helping the counselee become aware of all the factors that would involve arriving at particular decision. Few would go beyond this.

During the interview, both the counselor and the counselee will communicate with each other in both a verbal and nonverbal manner. In other words, the counselee will be *inferring* the counselor's attitude from his/her speech and behavior, just as the counselor will be inferring the counselee's attitude. If we accept this, then two generalizations become possible. First, the counselor must demonstrate his/her acceptance, sincerity, and understanding to the counselee. You can't just tell a person that you are interested in him/her and that you wish to help. This must be demonstrated. A recent incident involved a reticent student who so frustrated the counselor that he leaned across the table and shouted, "Look, John, you've got to trust me—I'm here to help you!" The importance of each word was emphasized by accompanying slaps on the table.

A second area of importance is the counselor's sensitivity as he/she communicates with the counselee. We are not recommending that you stare at the counselee so that you "don't miss a thing!" or that you hang on the importance of "every little word." We are hoping that you recognize observation as a skill to develop, and that you see the importance of concentrating on the counselee and what he/she is saying.

OPENING THE INTERVIEW The counselor should acknowledge the counselee's responsibility for selecting the initial topic of conversation. This can be done by asking the counselee what he/she would like to discuss, how he/she happened to come to the counselor, or what's on his/her mind?

The counselor has the responsibility for establishing limits in counseling as to topics to be discussed and the intensity with which they are to be treated. Both the counselor and the counselee have the responsibility for deciding on how much time should be spent during the interview, on the various topics, or when new topics or problems should be introduced. In general, interviews are limited to forty-five minutes and should be terminated when the time is up. This does not mean that you should close the interview abruptly. Rather, you should bring the interview to a leisurely close.

The relationship between you and the counselee begins as soon as you meet one another. Many counselees are ready to discuss their concerns when they begin to talk with a counselor; others are more comfortable if they spend a short time becoming acquainted with the counselor. The initial introductory conversation need not and should not extend through a large part of the interview. Counselees feel most satistied when they and the counselor can begin to talk about the topics at hand soon after the beginning of the interview. Comments about the weather or the counselor's regret that the counselee had to wait a few minutes usually are enough to create a relaxed atmosphere.

During the initial interview, get acquainted by listening—don't probe or press for important decisions. Help the counselee improve his/her own planning—don't mastermind the case or try to find out "just what is the problem." Make this a safe place to explore some ideas—not a place for cross-examination. Develop any potentially good topic that arises—even if it wasn't your idea. Keep the focus on the *counselee* and what he/she wants to talk about, not on what *you* feel is important. Remember that the counselee is the most important person in the counseling process and that you aren't going to solve all his/her problems in one session.

Sometime during the initial interview, not necessarily at the very beginning, you should go over such items as: length of interview (forty-five minutes), observation and taping of interviews, confidentiality, report to schools, and the number of times the counselee can return (as often as he/she feels necessary).

PURPOSES AND GOALS FOR THE INTERVIEW The counseling interview must have a purpose, and the goals for the interview must be limited. The counselor's goals are restricted, and he/she hopes that whatever the counselee learns in the counseling interview will perhaps influence certain other aspects of his/her life. During the interview, the counselor and counselee should not continually move from one objective or topic to another. Neither one is going to solve all the world's problems in one or two sessions—especially if the counselor wishes any of the learning that takes place to remain with the counselee. It is important to understand that in most cases, the problems or decisions that may be facing the counselee have been developing for a considerable time and will be affecting a considerable portion of his/her life. When placed within the context of a life span, then, the time a counselee spends with you occupies a relatively short space.

An outside time limit of forty-five minutes is placed on interviews at the laboratory, not from research evidence that this is the optimum amount of time, but in order to maintain an orderly and realistic time schedule. However, do not feel bound to this time limit by either extending the interview to "fill the time" or to keep the counselee talking. If you do extend the interview beyond the point of accomplishment, your counselee may come to wonder, "What's going on?" Indeed, there is some evidence that the shorter, more emphatic, to-the-point interview will aid the counselee toward making more progress than would the extended, rambling type of interview.

At this point, you may feel frustrated with conflicting admonitions (e.g., "Take your time, but don't take too much time"). It might, then, be well to touch on what could be termed counselor judgment. In short, this factor is what sets counseling apart as a profession: the need for the professional to use good judgment in order to determine his/her actions at a particular time. If counseling were a mechanistic technique, we would have no claim to professional identity.

PACE IN THE INTERVIEW The pacing, or timing, of counseling is important. A session devoted to the careful discussion of one, two, or three topics may help the counselee to understand and learn. An hour crowded with discussion of six or more important topics may result in confusion and anxiety. Ideas presented too quickly, questions asked without adequate time to consider previous answers, and a rapid style of speaking may produce an interview which leaves the counselee breathlessly wondering what has been happening. A leisurely pace is usually most effective in counseling.

The use of silence during counseling often causes much anxiety in the beginning counselor. A few seconds of silence to a beginning counselor appears much longer than it really is. Consequently, you may feel compelled to speak or have the counselee speak throughout the entire period. The actual number of words spoken by either the counselor or counselee bears little relationship to the progress that may or may not be made in the interview. A period of silence extending through one or even more minutes during an interview may provide both participants with an opportunity to consider what they have been discussing, to think of new topics, and to try to organize their information and ideas. *The most active counseling may occur in the mind of the counselee during these periods of silence.*

VOCABULARY If communication is to be effective, the counselor must use words that are understood by the counselee and have the same meaning that they have for himself. It is well to remember that to each of us words in and of themselves are unique conveyors of ideas and feelings. The counselor must become sensitive to what the counselee is attempting to communicate. A recent book entitled, *My Language Is Me* conveys the idea that an individual expresses him/herself through a personal language pattern. The vocabulary you use must be within the comprehension of the counselee. You must also remember that the counselee may attach meaning to words which are not what you assume. Be particularly careful to avoid using technical and professional terms.

TO ADVISE OR NOT You frequently have to decide when to advise and when to refrain from advising counselees, particularly when they ask such questions as, "What would you do if you were me?" Whether or not to advise depends on the persons involved *and* the type of advice requested. The counselor's experience and knowledge should be made available to the counselee, but *only* insofar as the counselee is able to incorporate this into his/her own decision making. Again, our goal in counseling is not to make decisions for the counselee, but to *aid* him/her in making his/her own decisions now and in the future. Viewed in the perspective of helping the client become capable of self-guidance in the future, we can appreciate the importance of helping the counselee learn new methods of problem solving. Remember, counseling is a learning process, not a giving of advice.

CLOSING THE INTERVIEW You, as a counselor, may have some anxiety as you near the end of an interview. Instead of stopping your counselee abruptly, it may be helpful to mention casually that there are a few minutes remaining in the session. At this time, the counselee may bring up a new topic. Nevertheless, you should hold to the time limit.

Have the client summarize the interview *only if you feel it will benefit him/her*.

Try to end an interview on a positive note—even though some of it was unpleasant. The decision to return for another interview must always remain with the counselee, although you should demonstrate your willingness to work with the counselee as long as necessary.

GROUP MEETINGS During the counseling practicum, the focus should be on *your* development as a counselor. An atmosphere conducive to self-evaluation and constructive criticism should be provided throughout the course in the seminar sessions. As recorded interviews are being evaluated, each counselor should make notes and question procedures utilized. Following are some questions to think about:

1. Is the counselor attempting to understand and empathize with the counselee?
2. Is *rapport* being developed?
3. What is being *accomplished*?
4. Are the counselor's statements serving to *clarify* and *reflect* the counselee's feelings?
5. Is the counselor *dominating* the interview? To what *purpose*?
6. Is the counselor able to handle *feeling*?
7. Are tests that are being administered serving a *purpose*, or are they being utilized as a "crutch"?
8. What *progress* is being made? Is this in line with what the counselee wants?

INTERVIEW LOGS Experience has shown that it is highly desirable to make a written summary of interviews immediately following the session. It is strongly recommended that you adopt this procedure.

SELF-EVALUATION Self-evaluation should include an evaluation of *your* progress. What strengths do you see? What weaknesses need to be worked on? Substantiate this by references to your interview experiences.

Included also should be a statement of your personal approach to, and philosophy of, counseling. What has influenced your development? What progress have you made? What reading has helped you and influenced you?

REPORT WRITING Following the termination of each contact, a summary report should be prepared. The formal reports on individual counselees are a necessary part of the counseling process for the following reasons:

1. To facilitate communication and cooperative effort with the agencies and school systems from which the counselees come.
2. To facilitate communication and cooperative effort with the community agencies and other professional groups involved with the counselee.
3. To maintain a written record of findings and recommendations for future reference and use.

To satisfy the objective of clear communication, the language of the report should:

1. Avoid technical psychological and educational terms.
2. Employ concise phrases, simple sentences, and brief paragraphs.
3. Use the same tense of the verb throughout the report.
4. Use impersonal nouns and third-person references.
5. Employ modifiers or qualifying phrases to indicate the tentative nature of the generalizations and conclusions.

Each summary must be approved by the supervisor. It is recommended that a rough draft be prepared first and then reviewed with the supervisor.

CONFIDENTIALITY AND ETHICS Throughout counseling, counselors must make decisions concerning their actions and the probable effects of these actions on their counselees. It may seem pertinent to note that the first responsibility of counselors is to maintain their own mental health so that they may provide the best possible help to their counselees. The responsibilities, personal and occupational pressures, and emotional conflicts faced by counselors in day-to-day activities often constitute a serious problem. Not only must counselors be aware of their own personality biases which may distort their perception of others, but they must be aware of the general state of their mental health and realize when their "tensions are showing." In practical terms, if a counselor is upset or angry, he/she should make sure it does not interfere with the counseling relationship; otherwise he/she should cancel all appointments. This points up the advisability of the counselor having someone to talk to about his/her problems. This may be a colleague, spouse, or friend. The point is, "Know thyself—and talk it out when you feel the need." Further, remember that the counselor's first responsibility is to him/herself and he/she is not to spend leisure hours "on the job." He/She should endeavor to leave the problems of others—and the job—at the office.

A further ethical responsibility of the counselor is to be aware of his/her limitations. The school counselor, in the majority of cases, is neither a therapist nor a psychologist. Consequently, he/she should not attempt to deal with severe emotional problems or with deep-seated conflicts. In addition, the counselor should not attempt to "probe" for problems with what constitutes a captive audience. It is not the existence of the problem that is important, but the individual's realization that he/she needs help in order to cope. For example, high school students often have conflicts with their parents. This is *not* the business of the counselor unless the student brings this up and asks for help. One further aspect: the counselor should not counsel an individual who is being seen by another professional worker without consulting with the other professional.

Because the counselor is not trained, in most cases, in the use of individual psychological instruments, he/she should refrain from the use of personality and intelligence tests that require special training. These include the Stanford-Binet, Rorschach, TAT, and MMPI.

Throughout counseling, the counselor must make decisions about what effect certain actions will have on his/her counselees. It is the counselor's responsibility to make decisions concerning the release of information obtained during an interview. When a counselor reports information to others, it should be done only after considering all the implications and alternatives. When to communicate information, to whom it should be given, and the manner of communication should be based on the predicted outcomes. This information can have an effect on the lives of counselees.

Counseling information should never be a topic of social conversation or discussed with colleagues outside of a professional and private setting, and should never be used to enhance the counselor's status or prestige.

Confidentiality of information also depends on the policies and procedures set up for maintaining counseling records. The counselor's personal records are not "public records" maintained for official or public use. Counseling records should be available only to counselors; when information in these records is to be communicated to others, it should be interpreted by counselors. Further, conversations and records should always be sent out with the full knowledge and consent of the counselee. For these reasons stress should be placed on the following rules:

1. Be careful not to discuss clients in public. You can never be sure who may be nearby.
2. You should not take client folders home. You may take them out of the laboratory in order to organize them and bring them up-to-date, review pertinent material, etc. You are cautioned not to leave these where they may be seen by others (waiting area, classrooms, etc.). Do not ask for materials when clients are in the reception area.
3. Reports to schools, agencies, etc., should be approved by one of the instructors before they are sent out. A copy of whatever communication is sent must be placed in the client's folder.

The counselor is often faced with conflicts in his/her responsibilities. When one considers that the counselor has responsibilities to his/her counselees, their parents, the institution in which he/she is employed, and to his/her profession, the magnitude of these conflicts becomes clear. Suffice it to say that the counselor's primary responsibility — indeed, his/her reason for being — is to his/her counselees. Within limits set by the situation, the counselor should do everything in his/her power to protect counselees and see that no harm comes to them.

It is strongly recommended that all counselors familiarize themselves with the *ethical standards* of the APGA and/or the APA.

PROFESSIONAL GROWTH The responsibilities a person accepts as a counselor are serious. Some of the situations a counselor will encounter will undoubtedly have some effect on his/her morale. This brings up the question of how a counselor develops and maintains a satisfactory feeling toward his/her work which will assist him/her in providing an effective and competent service. Each counselor must, of course, answer this question for him/herself.

It is worthy of note that the major responsibility for growth rests with the counselor. He/she should ask, "Am I developing a counseling style which is:

1. Compatible with my own personal makeup and beliefs?
2. Compatible with general principles of counseling practice?
3. Compatible with the role I will be called upon to practice?"

A counselor will find him/herself progressing through stages of understanding his/her counselees during the course of the practicum somewhat as follows:

Level 1: Counseling is the same as teaching *or* social conversation *or* advice giving.

Level 2: Counseling consists of giving sympathy *or* support to the counselee.

Level 3: Counseling consists of sitting back and just listening to the words of the counselee.

Level 4: Counseling consists of the counselor's repeating the verbal content of the counselee's statements.

Level 5: Counseling includes the counselor's recognizing the underlying feeling expressed by the counselee in his/her statements.

Level 6: The counselor begins to reflect some of the feeling expressed by the counselee.

Level 7: The counselor consistently empathizes with his/her counselee and communicates this understanding to the counselee.

Level 8: The counselor not only reflects, but clarifies, the feelings expressed by the counselee and helps him/her gain greater self-understanding and insight. Then the counselor aids the client in clarifying alternatives and making decisions.

Progress is apt to be slow before you gain insight into your own feelings and motivations as a counselor. You should then progress through at least several levels listed above during the course of the practicum. This progress will come as a result of your efforts, for a counselor is not made. We can—and will—help you to become a counselor.

As a counselor, you will need to be socially sensitive, flexible, and imaginative, with control of your intellect and emotions. Achieving this can be a lifetime process, but by continuous self-scrutiny during the practicum experience, you should be able to develop a high level of understanding and acceptance of who you are and what you can do. We hope your professional human relationships will help you to see your own potential and your own adequacy.

As new methods, procedures, techniques, and principles are discovered in counseling, counselors must acquire them and learn to apply them. The training of a counselor is never completed; his/her professional responsibilities require that he/she read extensively, attend professional meetings to learn of new developments, and associate with those in the profession to learn of new opinions and techniques. The counselor should support his/her national, state, and local guidance associations; the benefits derived are well worth the cost.

As part of your professional growth and development in the counseling practicum, you are expected to read widely. Relate results of your reading to your work and ask questions about problems you may have; much can be learned through the sharing of experiences.

TESTING Tests can help to provide a better understanding of the counselee. Tests can, further, provide an assessment of a counselee's aptitudes, achievements, interests, values, and personality. However, you should be aware of the limitations of tests and make sure that the importance of tests not be overemphasized. Remember, the primary emphasis *must* be on the counselee's purposes, plans, feelings, needs, and problems, not on test results. The test results themselves are of little importance; the counselee's reaction to them and their meaning is our concern.

You may ask yourself when tests should be used. Tests may be used in long-range career and educational planning. We must not think that a few tests and an interview are enough to give vocational guidance. Further, tests should be brought into the counseling process smoothly, *as the need for objective evidence arises.* Tests are not the answer to all problems.

Tests may also be used to help your counselee with social growth and maturity. This type of testing involves the release and acceptance of feelings, clarifications and acceptance of self-concepts, and an understanding of personal values. It can also lead to clearer purposes and fuller expression on the part of the counselee. Testing is the process of the student finding his/herself or becoming. This takes time and skill in counseling.

If you find during the counseling interview that your counselee feels that tests are instrumental to the solution of his/her problems, go ahead and use them. The process of test selection may be a cooperative one shared by you and your client. Together you should decide if a test of interest, aptitude, achievement, or self-inventory would be most valuable. You may also mention the tests which are most accurate for obtaining the prediction desired.

As you interpret test results, describe in nontechnical language the predictions the counselee can expect of him/herself. Use the following examples to help you in the interview.[2]

Relate test data to other experiences—*don't* discuss them as abstractions.

Try: "How does this fit in with your interests as you know them?"
Not: "That's the way your interests look. Any questions?"

Make alternate plans sound respectable—*not* as impending failure.

Try: "If that doesn't happen to work out, what else could you try?"
Not: "Everything seems to point to law as your most likely career."

Reflect a student's rejection of low test scores—*don't* write off low performance.

---

[2]Adapted from material prepared by NDEA Institute enrollees.

Try: "You don't think this is your real ability?"
Not: "Tests aren't foolproof. There might have been a slip-up."

Get students involved in test interpretation—*don't* just recite the results.

Try: "What did you think of that test?" "How do you suppose you did?"
Not: "On this test you are at the 46th percentile. On this one, the 23rd percentile."

Explain the purpose of the test in functional terms—*not* in psychological jargon.

Try: "This test allows you to compare yourself with high school juniors in how well you can do math."
Not: "This DAT test, like the SCAT, measures numerical perception."

Distinguish carefully between interest and aptitude—*don't* use the terms loosely.

Try: "Now, this is interest (what you like); not aptitude (what you might be able to do)."
Not: "This test shows where your interests and aptitudes lie."

Use test results for student planning—*not* for the counselor's diagnosis.

Try: "This allows you to compare yourself with other seniors in ability to learn."
Not: "This confirms my hunch that you would be able to succeed in college."

Refresh the student's memory on each test before discussing it—*don't* discuss it cold.

Try: "Remember this is one on which you chose which things you liked best and least?"
Not: "On the Kuder you were high on persuasive and mechanical, low on artistic."

Let tests add to a student's picture of him/herself—*not* be a mysterious magic formula.

Try: "Add this test information to everything else you know about yourself."

Not: "According to these tests you should go to college and study law or journalism."

Relate scholastic aptitude to school record—*don't* look only at test results.

Try: "According to your ability you should be able to do A or B work with average effort."

Not: "Your grades haven't been good, but you have high aptitude for college."

Express low test performance or unpleasant information honestly—but with perspective.

Try: "You are within the range of successful college students but well below average."

Not: "Only 20 percent of college students have less scholastic ability than you."

Explain test results simply—*don't* use elaborate statistical devices.

Try: "This is high, this is low, this is average for seniors; here is about how you stand."

Not: "You fall within these fiducial limits. If you flip a coin 100 times, etc."

Turn the test profile sheets toward the student so that he/she can read them.

Try: (Read profile upside down yourself or follow along on a duplicate copy.)

Not: "Let's see if we can both read this profile." (This will necessitate both twisting to read the copy.)

Clearly establish interests as preferences—*don't* confuse them with ability.

Try: "You seem to like these activities, dislike those. Does this agree with the way you see yourself?"

Not: "You are high in social service, low in mechanical.'

Remember expressed and demonstrated interests—*not* just interest inventory results.

Try: "This inventory gives you another kind of picture of your interests."

Not: "This inventory will show where your interests lie."

In interpreting tests, predictions should be minimized. Rather than telling the student that he/she will succeed or fail in a particular field, it would be much better to indicate how his/her scores stand in relation to the scores of persons who go into the field and those who succeed or fail in those areas. A counselor cannot say from a test score, "You will be a success in college"; he/she simply does not know that much, even when the scores are very high. He/She *can* say, "Your scores on this college ability test are very much above average for entering college students. Students with scores such as yours usually succeed in college and make good marks."

In keeping with the importance of the goals of self-understanding and maturity in counseling, the counselee must be given adequate opportunity and time to react, to talk through, and to plan as test scores are explained. Remember, the counselee's reaction *to,* and perception *of* the test scores are more important than the results! The counselor should avoid explaining statistics, validities, reliabilities, etc., which have little meaning to the counselee even though they are important to the counselor.

A primary rule to be followed is that the client must be involved in the test interpretation session if it is to be meaningful. A thought for the counselor to keep in mind is that test results can and should be a vehicle that will enable self-exploration and self-understanding to take place. Thus, it is strongly suggested that a leisurely pace be followed in test interpretation sessions. Too often the interview becomes a hurried recitation of results with an ending of, "What do we do now?"

USE OF OCCUPATIONAL AND EDUCATIONAL INFORMATION

Information is necessary for all of us in order to make valid decisions about ourselves. In this regard, occupational-educational information can be of great value in helping counselees realistically appraise their world and to select and move toward individual goals. This does not mean that it is up to you to "make sure" that each counselee reads through the occupational file, but to be aware that such information can be extremely useful in counseling.

One cardinal rule stands out in regard to the use of information: "Study of self must precede study of occupations." The implications of this lead to the practice of a counselee being helped to examine his/her attitudes, values, goals, strengths, and weaknesses before examining the information. In other words, it is not a process of a counselee randomly looking through information in search of a career, but, rather, having an idea of what to look for in terms of his/her own needs. We should also remember that with many adolescents, interest and maturity do not begin to develop until the late teens. Consequently, counselees must often "tread the line" between the extremes of making no career choices and prematurely committing themselves. This can often lead to a counselee being helped to make several alternate or tentative choices rather than trying to make a definite career choice.

CAREER COUNSELING Career and vocational counseling is one of the most neglected areas of guidance and counseling. One reason is that too many counselors feel uncomfortable and insecure in attempting to help clients to plan their future. The goal that we should be striving for is to help our clients reach a level of career maturity so that they will be able to make future career decisions on their own. This is critically important since it is estimated that each individual entering the labor force will change occupations between six to eight times in his/her working career.

Again, the primary rule to be followed: *Study of self must precede study of occupations.* What does this mean in actual practice? First, the client must be helped to understand him/herself in terms of what is important to him/her (values), what he/she likes to do (interests), and what his/her strengths and weaknesses are (abilities). Then the counselee can be helped to relate these to the occupational world through exploration of resources such as the *Occupational Outlook Handbook*.

In the interview itself, care must be taken that information is brought into the process smoothly, as part of counseling, and not abruptly as an event to be "gotten over with." Only if we view occupational planning as a series of decisions influenced by an individual's perception of him/herself as a worker will we see the necessity for leisurely consideration of all important factors involved in choosing a career. Consequently, a discussion of careers may extend over a series of interviews in which the counselee is helped to clarify his/her self-concept, what he/she wants from a career, and how he/she can progress toward chosen goals

REFERENCES

1. Adams, James Frederick.
   1965 *Counseling and Guidance: A Summary View.* New York: Macmillan.
2. Arbuckle, Dugald S.
   1970 *Counseling,* 2nd ed. Boston: Allyn and Bacon.
3. Arbuckle, Dugald S.
   1975 *Counseling and Psychotherapy,* 3rd ed. Boston: Allyn and Bacon.
4. Arbuckle, Dugald S.
   1967 *Counseling and Psychotherapy: An Overview.* New York: McGraw-Hill.
5. Arbuckle, Dugald S.
   1965 *Counseling: Philosophy, Theory and Practice.* Boston: Allyn and Bacon.
6. Ard, Ben N., ed.
   1966 *Counseling and Psychotherapy: Classics on Theories and Issues.* Palo Alto, Cal.: Science and Behavior Books.
7. Barclay, J.R.
   1971 *Foundations of Counseling Strategies.* New York: Wiley.
8. Beck, C.E.
   1971 *Philosophical Guidelines for Counseling.* Dubuque: Brown.
9. Benjamin, A.
   1974 *The Helping Interview,* 2nd ed. Boston: Houghton Mifflin.
10. Berdie, Ralph F.
    1958 "Program of Counseling Interview Research." *Educational and Psychological Measurement,* 18:255-274.
11. Bernard, Harold W., and Fullmer, Daniel W.
    1969 *Principles of Guidance: A Basic Text.* Scranton, Pa.: International Textbook Company.
12. Blocher, Donald H.
    1966 *Developmental Counseling.* New York: The Ronald Press.
13. Blocher, Donald H.
    1974 *Developmental Counseling,* 2nd ed New York: The Ronald Press.
14. Bordin, Edward S.
    1969 *Psychological Counseling,* 2nd ed. New York: Appleton-Century-Crofts, Educational Division, Meredith Corporation.
15. Boy, A., and Pine, G.
    1963 *Client-Centered Counseling in the Secondary School.* Boston: Houghton Mifflin.

Note: Credit for revising this bibliography is given to Cass Gaska.

16. Boy, Angelo V., and Pine, Gerald J.
1968 *The Counselor in the Schools: A Reconceptualization.* Boston: Houghton Mifflin

17. Brammer, L.M.
1973 *The Helping Relationship.* Englewood Cliffs: Prentice-Hall.

18. Brammer, Lawrence, and Shostrom, Everett.
1968 *Therapeutic Psychology: Fundamentals of Actualization, Counseling and Psychotherapy,* 2nd ed. Englewood Cliffs, N.J.: Prentice-Hall

19. Buchheimer, A., and Balogh, S.C.
1961 *The Counseling Relationship.* Chicago: Science Research Associates.

20. Byrne, R.H.
1963 *The School Counselor.* Boston: Houghton Mifflin.

21. Carkhuff, R.R., and Pierce, R.M.
1975 *The Art of Helping.* Amherst, Mass.: Human Resource Development Press.

22. Carkhuff, R.R.
1969 *Helping and Human Relations.* New York: Holt, Rinehart and Winston.

23. Cottle, W.C.
1973 *Beginning Counseling Practicum.* New York: Grune and Stratton.

24. Cottle, W.C., and Downie, N.M.
1970 *Preparation for Counseling.* Englewood Cliffs, N.J.: Prentice-Hall.

25. Davis, J.L., ed.
1973 *Counselors: Agents of Behavior and Social Change.* New York: MSS Information Company.

26. Delaney, D.J. and Eisenberg, S.
1977 *The Counseling Process.* Chicago: Rand McNally.

27. Dinkmeyer, Don C.
1968 *Guidance and Counseling in the Elementary School.* New York: Holt, Rinehart and Winston.

28. Downing, L.N.
1975 *Counseling Theories and Techniques.* Chicago: Nelson-Hall.

29. Downing, Lester N.
1968 *Guidance and Counseling Services: An Introduction.* New York: McGraw-Hill.

30. Dyer, W.W. and Vriend, J.
1975 *Counseling Techniques that Work.* Washington: APGA Press.

31. Elbert, E.J.
1971 *I Understand.* London: Sheed and Ward.

32. Erickson, C.E.
1950 *The Counseling Interview.* New York: Prentice-Hall.

33. Escobedo, A.E.
1974 *Chicano Counselor.* Dallas: Trucha.

34. Farwell, G.F. et al.
   1974 *The Counselors Handbook.* Scranton: Intext.
35. Faust, Verne.
   1968 *The Counselor-Consultant in the Elementary School.* Boston: Houghton Mifflin.
36. Frey, D.H. and Heslet, F.E.
   1975 *Existential Theory for Counselors.* Boston: Houghton Mifflin.
37. Froehlich, C.P. and Hoyt, K.B.
   1959 *Guidance Testing.* Chicago: Science Research Associates.
38. Fullmer, D.W., and Bernard, H.W.
   1964 *Counseling: Content and Process.* Chicago: Science Research Associates.
39. Gazda, G.M., ed.
   1975 *Basic Approaches to Group Psychotherapy and Group Counseling,* 2nd ed. Springfield, Ill.: Thomas.
40. Hansen, James C. and Stevic, Richard R.
   1969 *Elementary School Guidance.* New York: Macmillan.
41. Hansen, J.C. and Cramer, S.H., eds.
   1971 *Group Guidance and Counseling in the Schools.* New York: Appleton-Century-Crofts.
42. Hansen, J.C., et al.
   1972 *Counseling: Theory and Process.* Boston: Allyn and Bacon.
43. Harms, Ernest, and Schreiber, Paul, eds.
   1963 *Handbook for Counseling Techniques.* New York: Pergamon Press.
44. Hill, George E., and Luckey, Eleanore Brown.
   1969 *Guidance for Children in the Elementary School.* New York: Appleton-Century-Crofts, Educational Division, Meredith Corporation.
45. Hill, G.E.
   1974 *Management and Improvement of Guidance.* Englewood Cliffs, N.J.: Prentice-Hall.
46. Kahn, Robert L., and Cannell, Charles F.
   1957 *The Dynamics of Interviewing.* New York: Wiley.
47. Kell, Bill L., and Mueller, William J.
   1966 *Impact and Change: A Study of Counseling Relationships.* New York: Appleton-Century-Crofts, Educational Division, Meredith Corporation.
48. Kell, B.L., and Burow, J.M.
   1970 *Developmental Counseling and Therapy.* Boston: Houghton Mifflin.
49. Krumboltz, J.D., and Thoresen, C.E., eds.
   1969 *Behavioral Counseling.* New York: Holt, Rinehart and Winston.
50. Krumboltz, John D., ed.
   1966 *Revolution in Counseling: Implications of Behavioral Science.* Boston: Houghton Mifflin.
51. Lewis, E.C.
   1970 *The Psychology of Counseling.* New York: Holt, Rinehart and Winston.

52. Loughary, John W.
 1961 *Counseling in Secondary Schools.* New York: Harper and Brothers.
53. McDaniel, H.B.
 1956 *Guidance in the Modern School.* New York: Dryden Press.
54. McGowan, J F., and Schmidt, L.D.
 1962 *Counseling: Readings in Theory and Practice.* New York: Holt, Rinehart and Winston.
55. McKinney, F.
 1958 *Counseling for Personal Adjustment.* Boston: Houghton Mifflin.
56. Munson, H.L.
 1971 *Foundations of Developmental Guidance.* Boston: Allyn and Bacon.
57. Muro, J.J.
 1970 *The Counselor's Work in the Elementary School.* Scranton: Intext.
58. Nelson, R.C.
 1972 *Guidance and Counseling in the Elementary School.* New York: Holt, Rinehart and Winston.
59. Ohlsen, M.M., ed.
 1973 *Counseling Children in Groups.* New York: Holt, Rinehart and Winston.
60. Ohlsen, Merle M.
 1964 *Guidance Services in the Modern School.* New York: Harcourt, Brace and World.
61. Okun, B.F.
 1976 *Effective Helping.* Scituate, Mass.: Duxbury.
62. Oman, J.B.
 1973 *Group Counseling in the Church.* Minneapolis, Minn.: Augsburg.
63. Osipow, S.H., and Walsh, W.B.
 1970 *Strategies in Counseling for Behavior Change.* New York: Appleton-Century-Crofts.
64. Patterson, Cecil H.
 1967 *The Counselor in the School.* New York: McGraw-Hill.
65. Patterson, C.H.
 1973 *Theories of Counseling and Psychotherapy,* 2nd ed. New York: Harper and Row.
66. Peters, H.J., and Shertzer, B.
 1969 *Guidance,* 2nd ed. Columbus: Merrill.
67. Peters, Herman J., and Farwell, Gail F.
 1967 *Guidance: A Developmental Approach.* Chicago: Rand McNally.
68. Peters, H.J., and Shertzer, B.
 1974 *Guidance: Program Development and Management,* 3rd ed. Columbus: Merrill.
69. Peters, H.J.
 1970 *The Guidance Process.* Itasca, Illinois: F.E. Peacock.
70. Peters, Herman J., and Bathory, Michael J.
 1968 *School Counseling Perspectives and Procedures.* Itasca, Ill.: F.E. Peacock

71. Porter, E.H.
    1950 *Introduction to Therapeutic Counseling.* Boston: Houghton Mifflin.
72. Raimy, V.
    1971 *The Self-Concept as a Factor in Counseling and Personality Organization.* Columbus: Ohio State University Press.
73. Richardson, H.D., and Baron, M.
    1975 *Developmental Counseling in Education.* Boston: Houghton Mifflin.
74. Robinson, Francis P.
    1950 *Principles and Procedures in Student Counseling.* New York: Harper and Brothers.
75. Rogers, Carl R.
    1942 *Counseling and Psychotherapy.* Boston: Houghton Mifflin.
76. Rothney, J.W.M.
    1972 *Adaptive Counseling in Schools.* Englewood Cliffs, N.J.: Prentice-Hall.
77. Ryan, C.W.
    1975 *Career Education,* 3rd ed. Boston: Houghton Mifflin.
78. Sachs, Benjamin M.
    1966 *The Student, The Interview and The Curriculum.* Boston: Houghton Mifflin.
79. Shertzer, Bruce, and Stone, Shelley C.
    1968 *Fundamentals of Counseling.* Boston: Houghton Mifflin.
80. Shertzer, B. and Stone, S.C.
    1971 *Fundamentals of Counseling,* 2nd ed. Boston: Houghton Mifflin.
81. Shertzer, B. and Stone, S.C.
    1976 *Fundamentals of Guidance,* 3d ed. Boston: Houghton Mifflin.
82. Shostrom, Everett, and Brammer, Lawrence.
    1952 *Dynamics of the Counseling Process.* New York: McGraw-Hill.
83. Sweeney, T.J.
    1975 *Adlerian Counseling.* Boston: Houghton Mifflin.
84. Thompson. C.L., and Poppen, W.A.
    1972 *For Those Who Care.* Columbus: Merrill.
85. Thompson. S., and Kahn, J.H.
    1970 *The Group Process as a Helping Technique.* London: Pergamon.
86. Tolbert, E.L.
    1971 *Introduction to Counseling.* New York: McGraw-Hill.
87. Truax, Charles B., and Carkhuff, Robert R.
    1967 *Toward Effective Counseling and Psychotherapy: Training and Practice.* Chicago: Aldine.
88. Tyler, Leona E.
    1969 *The Work of the Counselor,* 3rd ed. New York: Appleton-Century-Crofts.

89. Van Hoose, William H.
    1968 *Counseling in the Elementary School.* Itasca, Ill.: F.E. Peacock.
90. Van Hoose, W.H., et al.
    1970 *The Elementary School Counselor,* 2nd ed. rev. Detroit: Wayne State University Press.
91. Van Kaam, Adrian L.
    1966 *The Art of Existential Counseling.* Wilkes-Barre, Pa.: Dimension Books.
92. Vriend, J., and Dyer, W.W., eds.
    1973 *Counseling Effectively in Groups.* Englewood Cliffs, N.J.: Educational Technology.
93. Williamson, E.G.
    1950 *Counseling Adolescents.* New York: McGraw-Hill.
94. Wreen, C.G.
    1973 *The World of the Contemporary Counselor.* Boston: Houghton Mifflin.
95. Woody, R.H.
    1971 *Psychobehavioral Counseling Therapy.* New York: Appleton-Century-Crofts.

Informational Resources on Counseling

1. Opening the Interview
  4. Arbuckle, pp. 327-334, revised.
  9. Benjamin, pp. 11-14.
  11. Bernard and Fullmer, p. 260.
  18. Brammer and Shostrom, pp. 192-194.
  19. Buchheimer and Balogh, pp. 1-15, 17-51.
  32. Erickson, p. 32.
  37 Froehlich and Hoyt, pp. 266-271.
  43 Harms and Schreiber, pp. 97-99, 485.
  47 Kell and Mueller, pp. 5-7, 20-33.
  60 Ohlsen, pp. 105-115.
  67. Peters and Farwell, p. 222.
  71. Porter, pp. 88-122.
  78. Sachs, pp. 10-34.

Appendix 193

79. Shertzer and Stone, p. 361.
88. Tyler, pp. 49-53.
93. Williamson, pp. 225-227.

2. Phrasing Questions
4. Arbuckle, pp. 192-198.
9. Benjamin, pp. 80-87.
16. Boy and Pine, pp. 65-67, 203-204.
37. Froehlich and Hoyt, pp. 275-276
52. Loughary, pp. 46-61.
70. Peters and Bathory, pp. 178-182.
71. Porter, pp. 11-14, 62-77
78. Sachs, pp. 24-34.
79. Shertzer and Stone, pp. 364-365.
88. Tyler, pp. 39-42, 158-172.

3. The Counselee's Experience with the Counselor
4. Arbuckle, pp. 63-84, 339-384.
10. Berdie, pp. 260-261.
32. Erickson, pp. 144-145.
42. Hansen, pp. 52-54, 64.
59. Ohlsen, pp. 6-ff.
60. Ohlsen, pp. 115-126.
71. Porter, p. 101.
75. Rogers, pp. 149-151.
82. Shostrom and Brammer, pp. 47-168.

4. Overtalking the Counselee
9. Benjamin, pp. 101-102.
37. Froehlich and Hoyt, pp. 267-268.
60. Ohlsen, pp. 105-140.
73. Richardson and Baron; p. 20.
88. Tyler, pp. 38-42.

5. Accepting the Counselee's Attitudes and Feelings
4. Arbuckle, pp. 57-190.
11. Bernard and Fullmer, p. 2-3.
15. Boy and Pine, pp. 32-33, 49-51, 135-136.
16. Boy and Pine, pp. 130, 151-152, 209.
18. Brammer and Shostrom, pp. 173-178.

21. Carkhuff and Pierce, p. 26.
37. Froehlich and Hoyt, pp. 275-276.
55. McKinney, pp. 18, 288.
59. Ohlsen, pp 83 - 92.
64. Patterson, pp. 230-231.
67. Peters and Farwell, p. 235.
71. Porter, pp. 11-14, 62-77, 149-150.
75. Rogers, pp. 133-148.
79. Shertzer and Stone, pp. 344-346.
81. Shertzer and Stone, pp. 5, 17, 34.
88. Tyler, pp. 33-38, 49-63, 142, 147-149, 195-196, 199-200, 217-228.
92. Vriend and Dyer, p. 160.
94. Wrenn, p. 4.

6. Cross-examining
9. Benjamin, pp. 72-74.
10. Berdie, p. 50.
42. Hansen, p. 262.
46. Kahn and Cannell, pp. 187-188, 205-208, 212.
71. Porter, p. 198.

7. Silences in the Interview
5. Arbuckle, pp. 198-199.
9. Benjamin, pp. 24-26, 89, 102.
12. Blocher, pp. 32-34.
18. Brammer and Shostrom, pp. 211-216.
37. Froehlich and Hoyt, p. 277.
55. McKinney, p. 288.
60. Ohlsen, pp. 109-112.
75. Rogers, pp. 165-167.
79. Shertzer and Stone, pp. 373-375.
88. Tyler, pp. 40-42.

8. Reflecting the Counselee's Feeling
5. Arbuckle, pp. 208-220.
9. Benjamin, pp. 117-119.
15. Boy and Pine, pp. 15-16, 136.
18. Brammer and Shostrom, pp. 194-203.
55. McKinney, pp. 332, 343, 352.

60. Ohlsen, pp. 116-118.
71. Porter, pp. 11-44, 62-77.
79. Shertzer and Stone, pp. 363, 365-367.
87. Truax and and Carkhuff, p. 40.
88. Tyler, pp. 200-212.

9. Distribution of Talking Time
9. Benjamin, pp. 16-18, 29-31.
15. Boy and Pine, pp. 20-21, 28.
37. Froehlich and Hoyt, pp. 267-268.
60. Ohlsen, pp. 115-116.
75. Rogers, pp. 122-124.
88. Tyler, pp. 135-172.

10. The Vocabulary of the Interviewer
59. Ohlsen, p. 3.
71. Porter, pp. 63-84.
73. Richardson and Baron; pp. 9-10.
88. Tyler, pp. 38-42.
89. Van Hoose, p. 95.

11. Control of the Interview
18. Brammer and Shostrom, pp. 209-211.
32. Erickson, p. 80.
37. Froehlich and Hoyt, p. 279.
60. Ohlsen, pp. 115-116.
71. Porter, pp. 147-151.
81. Shertzer and Stone, p. 178.

12. Avoid the Personal Pronoun
15. Boy and Pine, pp. 138-172.
18. Brammer and Shostrom, pp. 198-200.
32. Erickson, p. 80.

13. Problems in the Interview
9. Benjamin, pp. 18-32.
12. Blocher, pp. 156-157.
32. Erickson, p. 81.
55. McKinney, p. 283.
88. Tyler, pp. 8-9, 41, 52-53, 55-57.

14. Setting Limits on the Interview
- *18.* Brammer and Shostrom, pp. 207-209, 221-222.
- *42.* Hansen, pp. 71, 285.
- *55.* McKinney, p. 234.
- *59.* Ohlsen, pp. 102-112.
- *70.* Peters and Bathory, pp. 34-35.
- *75.* Rogers, pp. 100-103.
- *79.* Shertzer and Stone, pp. 360-361.

15. Plans for Action
- *9.* Benjamin, p. 32.
- *12.* Blocher, pp. 157-159.
- *14.* Bordin, p. 269.
- *19.* Buchheimer and Balogh, pp. 86-107, 206-224.
- *21.* Carkhuff and Pierce, p. 3.
- *70.* Peters and Bathory, pp. 100-101.
- *71.* Porter, pp. 107-122, 131-132, 145-146, 179-180.
- *73.* Richardson and Baron, p. 20.
- *88.* Tyler, pp. 64-78.
- *92.* Vriend and Dyer, p. 56, 190.

16. Summarizing the Interview
- *9.* Benjamin, pp. 31-32, 115.
- *10.* Berdie, p. 262.
- *15.* Boy and Pine, p. 29.
- *18.* Brammer and Shostrom, pp. 225-226.
- *19.* Buchheimer and Balogh, pp. 109-166.
- *32.* Erickson, pp. 82, 91-92.
- *59.* Ohlsen, pp. 129-134.
- *75.* Rogers, pp. 33, 231.
- *79.* Shertzer and Stone, p. 363.
- *82.* Shostrom and Brammer, p. 149.

17. Ending the Interview
- *5.* Arbuckle, pp. 385-397.
- *9.* Benjamin, pp. 28-32.
- *18.* Brammer and Shostrom, pp. 222-230.
- *19.* Buchheimer and Balogh, pp. 103-107.
- *21.* Carkhuff and Pierce, p. 195.
- *37.* Froehlich and Hoyt, pp. 266, 287-289.

59. Ohlsen, pp. 3, 72, 332
60. Ohlsen, pp. 129-134.
70. Peters and Bathory, pp. 200-202.
71. Porter, pp. 107-122.
74. Robinson, pp. 154-155.
75. Rogers, pp. 220-228.
88. Tyler, pp. 170-172.

18. Structuring the Interview
9. Benjamin, pp. 16-18, 29-31.
12. Blocher, pp. 158-159.
14. Bordin, pp. 221-226.
15. Boy and Pine, pp. 28-29, 211-212.
37. Froehlich and Hoyt, pp. 260-289.
40. Hansen and Stevic, pp. 93-94.
44. Hill and Luckey, pp. 215-217.
52. Loughary, pp. 54-57.
59. Ohlsen, p. 5.
60. Ohlsen, pp, 115-116.
74. Robinson, pp. 26-34, 150-152.
79. Shertzer and Stone, pp. 359-361.
89. Van Hoose, pp. 89-91.

19. Counselor's Handling of Hostility (toward a teacher)
18. Brammer and Shostrom, pp. 42-43, 237-238, 242.
32. Erickson, pp. 28-29.
35. Faust, pp. 97-98.
42. Hansen, p. 71.
52. Loughary, p. 99.
60. Ohlsen, pp. 121-125.
71. Porter, p. 32.
75. Rogers, pp. 69-71, 150-151, 153-159, 234-235.
81. Shertzer and Stone, pp. 375, 446.
87. Truax and Carkhuff, pp. 266-271.

20. Counselee Wants a Direct Answer
9. Benjamin, pp. 74-78.
18. Brammer and Shostrom, p. 294.
60. Ohlsen, pp. 126-129.
75. Rogers, pp. 160-164.

198 The Authentic Counselor

81. Shertzer and Stone, p. 290.

21. Request for Test Interpretation
5. Arbuckle, pp. 257-264.
9. Benjamin, p. 96.
12. Blocher, pp. 135-136.
14. Bordin, pp. 263, 295-312, 315.
15 Boy and Pine, pp. 127-132, 135-136, 140-145.
3. Boy and Pine, p. 255.
18. Brammer and Shostrom, pp. 304-311.
27. Dinkmeyer, pp. 149-157.
29. Downing, pp. 122-123.
44. Hill and Luckey, pp. 173-176.
52. Loughary, pp. 95-99.
0. Ohlsen, pp. 218-245.
64. Patterson, pp. 278-282.
70. Peters and Bathory, pp. 172-177.
74. Robinson, pp. 188-191.
79. Shertzer and Stone, pp. 415-424.
81. Shertzer and Stone, p. 213.
88. Tyler, pp. 97-103.
89. Van Hoose, p. 77.

22. Play Media in Counseling
27. Dinkmeyer, pp. 267-270.
35. Faust, pp. 154-158.
40. Hansen and Stevic, pp. 97-100.
42. Hansen, p. 118.
44. Hill and Luckey, pp. 222-227.
59. Ohlsen, pp. 4-5, 35-37, 126-127.
70. Peters and Bathory, p. 167.
81. Shertzer and Stone, p. 300.
89. Van Hoose, pp. 96-97.
92. Vriend and Dyer, p. 226.

23. Clarification
9. Benjamin, pp. 87-89, 115-116, 130.
27. Dinkmeyer, pp. 257-258.
70. Peters and Bathory, p. 103.
79. Shertzer and Stone, p. 372.

24. Interpretaion
- 9. Benjamin, pp. 117, 119-121.
- 27. Dinkmeyer, p. 257.
- 59. Ohlsen, pp. 30-32.
- 67. Peters and Farwell, p. 109.
- 70. Peters and Bathory, pp. 102, 107.
- 79. Shertzer and Stone, pp. 369-372.

25. Reinforcement
- 9. Benjamin, pp. 126-128.
- 21. Carkhuff and Pierce, p. 141.
- 27. Dinkmeyer, pp. 236-239, 258.
- 40. Hansen and Stevic, pp. 94-97.
- 70. Peters and Bathory, p. 104.
- 87. Truax and Carkhuff, pp. 292-293.

26. Reluctant Participant
- 5. Arbuckle, pp. 196-199.
- 9. Benjamin, pp. 110-111.
- 50. Krumboltz, p. 110.
- 60. Ohlsen, pp. 105-115.
- 87. Truax and Carkhuff, pp. 292-293.

27. Ethical and Legal Procedures and Considerations
- 5. Arbuckle, pp. 278-291.
- 6. Ard, pp. 174-185.
- 9. Benjamin, pp. 52-56, 74.
- 16. Boy and Pine, pp. 39-43, 162-164.
- 38. Fullmer and Bernard, p. 32.
- 44. Hill and Luckey, pp. 232-235.
- 60. Ohlsen, pp. 140-144.
- 64. Patterson, pp. 447-463, 472-473.
- 70. Peters and Bathory, p. 122.
- 79. Shertzer and Stone, pp. 496-503.
- 80. Shertzer and Stone, pp. 147, 177.
- 89. Van Hoose, pp. 149-159.
- 94. Wrenn, p. 242.

28 Educational and Vocational Planning
- 5. Arbuckle, pp. 109-117

11. Bernard and Fullmer, pp. 268-284.
16. Boy and Pine, pp. 53-56.
29. Downing, pp. 182-197.
35. Faust, pp. 17-18, 184-185.
38. Fullmer and Bernard, p. 155.
40. Hansen and Stevic, p. 203.
43. Harms and Schreiber, pp. 81-82, 292-293.
44. Hill and Luckey, pp. 373, 377-380.
60. Ohlsen, pp. 19-20, 197, 319, 333-342, 421.
64. Patterson, pp. 241-263.
67. Peters and Farwell. p. 197.
70. Peters and Bathory, pp. 92, 419, 425.
89. Van Hoose, pp. 34, 83.
94. Wrenn, p. 200.

Index

Acceptance in the counseling relationship, 55–56
Accurate Empathy Scale, 62
Active listening, 63–64
Allen, Thomas W., 135
Altmann, H. A., 62, 134
Ambiguity, 104–20
  defined, 105–106
  importance of tolerance for, 118–19
  in counseling structure, 107–109
Ambivalence. *See* Ambiguity.
American Personnel and Guidance Association, 4
American Psychological Association, Division of Counseling Psychology, 4
Anderson, C. M., 21, 26
Anderson, Dervyn L., 62, 134

Arbuckle, Dugald S., 6–7, 74, 78, 138
Arnold, Dwight L., 141, 148, 167–68
Aspy, D., 62
Authentic behavior in counseling, 123–24, 130–42
  defined, 132–33
  dynamics, 137–41
  misrepresentation of, 123
  need for, 130–32
  self-disclosure, 133, 135–37

Balogh, Sara, 39–41
Bank, I., 23
Being and becoming, 157
Belkin, G. S., 138
Benjamin, Alfred, 63–64

Index

Berenson, Bernard G., 119, 139, 141
Black, H., 136
Blocher, Donald H., 7, 11, 13, 16, 60, 91, 105, 159
Bordin, Edward S., 112
Boyd, A. J., 31
Brammer, L. M., 80, 107
Brams, Jerome M., 118
Brooks, R. M., 27
Buber, M., 131
Buchheimer, Arnold, 39–41
Bundga, K. A., 136
Burow, Josephine M., 66

Callis, Robert, 113
Cameron, Norman, 37
Cannon, J. R., 134
Career counseling, 185
Carkhuff, R. A., 62
Carkhuff, Robert R., 20, 51, 60, 62, 66, 106, 119, 131-34, 139, 141
Carlson, J., 108
Chambers, J., 22
Children, counseling of, 57–59
Client
 expectations, 9–11
 growth, 37
 self-understanding, 113
 See also Counselee
Clifton, Robert, 124
Coleman, James C., 130–31
Colm, H., 140, 154
Combs, A. W., 21–22, 35–37, 39, 52, 134, 140, 156
Communication in the counseling relationship, 62–64
Confidentiality, 177–78
Conflicts, 37–38
Copeland, Elaine, 32–33
Counselee
 ambiguity in counseling, 107–109
 needs, 168–69
 resistance, 80–81, 90–91
 See also Client
Counseling
 according to self-concept, 31–33, 35, 39, 42, 112

classifying counselee, 154–55
conditions for, 20
defined, 4–6, 19
elements, 72–73, 78–79
establishing security, 91–97
goals, 6–13
historic antecedents, 2–4
ingredients of, 1–2
the interview, 168-69, 172–75
leads, 112
as learning process, 170–71, 174–75
need for, 2–3
process of, 12–16, 72–102
skills-building in 141
steps in, 98–101
tolerance of ambiguity, 104–20
toward decision-making, 43–45
transference in, 97–98
vocabulary, 174
See also Authentic behavior
Counseling Practicum, 166–85
Counseling relationship, 5
 acceptance of counselee, 55–56
 active listening in, 63–64
 characteristics, 50–55
 children in, 57–59
 communication in, 62–64
 counselor-client interaction, 51
 empathy and trust in, 60–62
 genuineness in counselor, 66
 rapport in, 55
 real, 66
 structuring, 65–66
 See also Counselor
Counselor
 attributes of, 66–67, 72–73
 being and becoming, 157
 certification, 3–4
 commitment to humaneness, 162
 domination of interview, 57
 genuineness, 141
 growth, 107, 179–80
 manipulation of counselee, 152
 as model, 162–63
 moral development, 160–62
 role playing, 158–59
 self-actualization, 148–52, 156–57, 159
 self-development, 167
 skill, 73–74

Index   **203**

transcendence of self, 159
values of, 74–76
view of counselee, 156
See also Counselor responsibility
Counselor responsibility
  for ambiguity, 106
  to counselee, 76–77, 178
  in counseling relationship, 78–79
  limitations of, 177
  to self, 157, 176–77
Culberson, J. O., 134
Cutler, R. L., 135

Daane, Calvin, 119
Darley, John G., 3
Decision-making, 43–45
Delaney, Daniel J., 13, 132, 137
Demos, George D., 133
Dey, G. R., 160
Dickenson, W. A., 62
Dies, R. R., 136
Dilley, J., 43–44
Dimick, K. M., 76, 79
Dolan, G. Keith, 119
Dreyfus, Edward, 152
Dunlop, Richard H., 10

Egan, G., 74
Ehrlich, H. J., 135
Eisenberg, L., 131
Eisenberg, Sheldon, 13, 132
Empathic Understanding Scale, 62
Empathy in the counseling
  relationship, 60–62
Esterson, A., 131
Ethics, 176–78
Experiential knowledge, 150–51

Farwell, Gail F., 137
Felker, D. W., 26

Ferguson, J. G., 100–101
Fiedler, Fred E., 52, 139
Fischer, J., 134
Foulds, Melvin L., 148
Frankl, Viktor E., 149
Frazier, A., 22
Freud, Sigmund, 3

Gale, R. F., 28, 30
Gazda, G., 138
Geist, M., 133
Gendlin, E. T., 133
Giannandrea, V., 136
Gitter, A. G., 136
Gladstein, Gerald A., 62
Goldstein, A. P., 90
Gonyea, G. G., 62
Goodstein, Leonard D., 75
Gordon, Thomas, 63
Gruberg, Ronald, 118

Hackney, H., 9
Haley, J., 131
Halikides, G., 133
Hansen, J. C., 138
Havighurst, R. J., 24
Hawkins, Sue, 58
Hayden, B., 134
Hendricks, G. C., 100–101
Hill, C., 7
Holland, Glen, 112
Holmes, D. S., 136
Horney, Karen, 34, 38
Hosford, Ray E., 11
Hountras, Peter T., 62, 133
Huff, V. E., 76, 79
Hurst, J. C., 75

Ince, Lawrence, 39
Interview, counseling, 168–69, 172–75

Jackson, M., 53
Jacobson, Lenore, 22
Jaffe, P. E., 136
Jersild, A. T., 26
Johnson, David W., 136
Jorgenson, G. T., 75
Jourard, Sidney M., 132, 136–37, 139, 152, 158

Kanner, L., 131
Katz, B., 62
Kazan, Elia, 131, 154
Kell, Bill L., 15, 66
Kelley, E. C., 149
Kennedy, John, 39
Kennedy, John F., 34
Kennedy, Robert, 34
King, Martin Luther, 34
Kinnick, Bernard, 119
Kohlberg, Lawrence, 160
Korman, A. K., 22
Kottler, J., 2, 4
Kratchovil, D., 62
Krumboltz, John D., 7–8, 119

Laing, R. D., 80, 131, 158–59
Landers, Ann, 104–105
Lecky, P., 33
Lee, D. E., 135
Leib, J. W., 148
LeMay, M. L., 148
Leonard, George E., 23, 149, 157
Lesser, W. M., 62
Levy, P. K., 136
Lieberman, L., 22
Lin, Tien-Teh, 137
Listening, active, 63–64
Loesch, L. C., 157
Lowther, M.A., 22

McDaniels, C., 22
McGreevy, C. Patrick, 119
Maier, Henry W., 55, 99–100

Manipulation of client, 152
Mann, Irene, 58
Mark, J. C., 131
Markman, Barry, 124
Maslow, Abraham, 28–30, 135, 154, 157, 159
May, P. O., 136
May, Rollo, 21
Mayer, G. Roy, 108
Meador, B. D., 138
Means, B. L., 61
Merrill, F. E., 26
Mezzano, J., 135
Mooney Problem Checklist, 9
Mueller, William T., 15
Murphy, K. C., 136

Nagel, E. H., 9
National Vocational Guidance Association, 3
Needs, hierarchy of, 28–30
Noonan, Patricia M., 136
Nye, S., 9

Passons, W. R., 160
Patterson, Cecil H., 8, 10, 13, 22, 61, 105
Perrone, P., 9
Peters, Herman J., 43, 137
Pierce, R. M., 74, 141
Pietrofesa, John J., 4, 21, 23, 73, 124
Ponzo, Z., 9
Practicum, 166–85
Professional standards, 158, 166–67

Robinson, Francis P., 64
Rogers, Carl R., 3–4, 13, 15–16, 33–34, 53, 56, 60, 63, 66, 107, 133, 138, 142, 151
Role playing, 158–59
Rosenthal, Robert, 22

Schauble, P. G., 74, 141
Self-actualization, defined, 147
    See also Counselor
        self-actualization
Self-actualizing person, 34–35
Self-concept, 21–27, 30–35, 39–41
Self-disclosure, 133, 135–37
Self-exploration, 8, 13–16
Self-identification, 5
Selfridge, F. F., 148
Self-understanding prior to decisions, 113
Shannon, Jack, 119
Shapiro, J. G., 133
Shertzer, Bruce, 9, 51, 65
Shostrom, E. L., 80, 107
Simonson, N. R., 136
Singer, M., 131
Skinner, B F., 160
Snyder, R. T., 22
Snyder, W. U., 148
Spiritas, A. A., 136
Spontaneity, 133
Staudenmeier, James J., 133
Stefflre, Buford, 4–5, 13, 77
Stone, Shelley C., 9, 51, 65
Strong, S. R., 136

Testing, 180–84
Thompson, C. L., 53, 136
Thorne, Frederick C., 32

Thorsen, C. E., 100–101
Tosi, Donald J., 136
Transference, 97–98
Traxler, A. E., 78
Truax, Charles B., 20, 51, 60, 62, 66, 106, 131–34
Trust in the counseling relationship, 60
Tyler, Leona E., 4, 12, 44–45, 113, 118, 122

Vander Kolk, C., 148
Van Hoose, William H., 2, 4, 58
Vocabulary, counseling, 174
Vriend, J., 73

Weikel, W. J., 157
Weiking, M. L., 9
Whitman, A., 132
Williamson, Edmund G., 3
World War II, influence on counseling, 3
Wrenn, C. Gilbert, 5

Zigon, F., 134
Zimmer, Jules, 39